ENNIS AND NANCY HAM LIBRARY
ROCHESTER COLLEGE
800 WEST AVON ROAD
ROCHESTER HILLS, MI 48307

ALSO BY
Carl L. Becker

Political Parties in the Province of New York from 1766–75 (1908)
Beginnings of the American People (1915)
Eve of the Revolution (1918)
Our Great Experiment in Democracy (1924)
The Declaration of Independence — A Study in the History of Political Ideas (1922, 1942)
The Spirit of '76 (*with G. M. Clark and W. E. Dodd*) (1926)
Modern History (1931)
The Heavenly City of the Eighteenth Century Philosophers (1932)
Every Man His Own Historian (1935)
Progress and Power (1936)
Story of Civilization (*with Frederic Duncalf*) (1938)
Modern Democracy (1941)
New Liberties for Old (1941)
Cornell University: Founders and the Founding (1943)
How New Will the Better World Be? (1944)

Freedom and Responsibility in the American Way of Life

THE WILLIAM W. COOK FOUNDATION was established at the University of Michigan to endow a distinguished Lectureship on American Institutions. The donor, William Wilson Cook, long a member of the New York bar, received the degree of Bachelor of Arts from the College of Literature, Science, and the Arts of the University in 1880, and the degree of Bachelor of Laws from the Law School in 1882. The lectures presented in this volume are the first in the series of lectures under the Foundation. They were delivered in the Rackham lecture halls at the University December 4 to 8, 1944, and are published, under a special arrangement between the University and the publisher, as the initial volume in the lectureship series.

FREEDOM AND RESPONSIBILITY

IN THE AMERICAN WAY OF LIFE

Five lectures delivered on the William W. Cook Foundation
at the University of Michigan, December 1944

By CARL L. BECKER

With an introductory essay by GEORGE H. SABINE
Vice President of Cornell University

GREENWOOD PRESS, PUBLISHERS
WESTPORT, CONNECTICUT

Library of Congress Cataloging in Publication Data

Becker, Carl Lotus, 1873-1945.
   Freedom and responsibility in the American way of life.

   Reprint of the ed. published by Knopf, New York, which was issued as v. 1 of the William W. Cook Foundation lectures.
   Includes index.
   1. Civil rights--United States--Addresses, essays, lectures. I. Title. II. Series: Michigan. University. William W. Cook Foundation. Lectures ; v. 1.
JC599.U5B35 1980   323.4'0973   80-11156
ISBN 0-313-22361-0 lib. bdg.

Copyright 1945 by Alfred A. Knopf, Inc. and by University of Michigan.

All rights reserved. No part of this book may be reproduced in any form without permission in writing from the publisher, except by a reviewer who may quote brief passages in a review to be printed in a magazine or newspaper.

Reprinted with the permission of Alfred A. Knopf, Inc.

Reprinted in 1980 by Greenwood Press, a division of Congressional Information Service, Inc., 51 Riverside Avenue, Westport, CT 06880

Printed in the United States of America

10 9 8 7 6 5 4 3 2 1

Preface

THIS SMALL VOLUME consists of five lectures delivered at the University of Michigan on the William W. Cook Foundation in December 1944. Except for a few minor changes made in response to valuable suggestions offered by persons who heard the lectures, and especially by Dean E. Blythe Stason of the University of Michigan Law School, the lectures are here printed in the form in which they were given.

Since I have published a number of articles and books dealing with various aspects of modern democracy and the political philosophy on which it rests, I found it impossible, in preparing some parts of these lectures, not to say again in substance what I had already said elsewhere, and in some paragraphs I have used the same phraseology, or very nearly the same, because it seemed to me that I could not make the point I had in mind so effectively in any other form. This applies to Lectures I and IV, in which I have used some parts of a lecture delivered at Cornell University and printed in *Safeguarding Civil Liberties Today* (Cornell University Press, 1945); to Lecture III, in which I have used some parts of a lecture delivered at the Lawrenceville School and printed in *Return to Freedom* (G. P. Putnam's Sons, 1944); and to Lecture V, in which I have used some parts of Chapter VI in *How New Will the Better World Be?* (Alfred A. Knopf, 1944). Permission to use matter previously published has been obtained from the publishers concerned.

For many courtesies extended to me at the time the lectures were given, I am much indebted to the Dean and faculty of the Law School, to the members of the Department of History, to the members of the committee of arrangements, and to many other members of the University faculty.

C. B.

Ithaca, N.Y.
January 13, 1945

The republican is the only form of government which is not eternally at open or secret war with the rights of mankind.

— THOMAS JEFFERSON

Contents

	Carl Lotus Becker	vii
I.	The American Political Tradition	1
II.	Freedom of Speech and Press	23
III.	Freedom of Learning and Teaching	44
IV.	Constitutional Government	65
V.	Private Economic Enterprise	89

CARL LOTUS BECKER was born in Blackhawk County, Iowa, September 7, 1873. At the time of his death in Ithaca, New York, April 10, 1945, approximately four months after delivering the lectures herein published, he was Professor Emeritus of History at Cornell University. The essay which follows is by George H. Sabine, Vice President of Cornell University and long a colleague of Becker on its faculty.

Carl Lotus Becker[1]

CARL BECKER united in a remarkable way the quality of incisive and critical intelligence with humanity of feeling and action. He had experienced in his own thought all the negative influences of modern scientific and philosophical criticism. He had subjected the intellectual framework of the democracy which he loved to the keenest and coolest analysis and had allowed his wit and irony to play over its illusions and its failures. He had found in the framework of the democratic tradition much that was traditional only, much that reflected the religion and the science and the morals of a day gone by, which could no longer endure the light of a maturer science and a new economy. With rare intellectual sensitivity he responded to all the currents of a changing social situation and a changing social thought, in an age when change was rapid and often destructive and when thought was likely to be directionless and conflicting. Yet his life and his thought were at all times molded by the humane ideals of the democratic tradition which he criticized and which his criticism placed among the lasting moral achievements of mankind. He lived and taught and wrote always in the faith that the great and valuable achievements of civilization are the products of intelligence and integrity and good will, to be won only in a society that gives free play to intelligence and good will against the pressure of mass emotion and conformity enforced by authority. For him the test of a civilized society was the degree in which law and public authority rest on free discussion and voluntary consent, and he valued democracy because, with all its faults, it still offered the widest scope for intelligence and good will.

[1] In revising this essay I have benefited by the comments of Professsor L. C. Petry, of the Cornell faculty, and Mr. E. R. B. Willis, of the Cornell University Library, both of whom had a longer and a more intimate acquaintance with Becker than I. G. H. S.

Introduction

In respect to these fundamental ideas there was little change or development in Becker's writing after he reached maturity. He extended his range and clarified his understanding and polished his style, but the direction of his interests and his native reactions changed little. Already in the brilliant essay on "Kansas" which he contributed in 1910 to the *Essays* dedicated to his teacher Turner, he described the frontier as a type of mind to be found in all places, the spirit of adventure and idealism; and "the Kansas spirit is the American spirit double distilled." Already it is the type of mind — closely related to what he later called the climate of opinion — that interested him: its individualism, idealism, moralism, intolerance, its determination to unite liberty with equality, and its faith in government — all to be understood as the spiritual reactions natural to a mode of living and a set of environing circumstances. His analysis and interpretation of the philosophy of natural rights in *The Declaration of Independence* is essentially identical with that which he gave ten years later in *The Heavenly City:* a new form of worship which "deified nature and denatured God." Again, what fascinated Becker was the transformation of old ideas under the impact of a new situation. His castigation of the triviality and sentimentality and provincialism of American politics, written at the end of the first World War, in *The United States, an Experiment in Democracy,* could easily be paralleled in the essays which he wrote near the close of his life under the spur of the second World War. All of Becker's work moves within a somewhat limited circle of ideas which recur again and again. Always he is interested in these as ideas, and in human beings as the creators and the bearers of ideas. For him the typical and the profoundly interesting and valuable part of human behavior lay in its ideal dimension — in the exercise of intelligence, in the endless effort to conform action to ideal principles, even in the creation of utopias and illusions which are the continual accompaniments of the process. In this he was perhaps as much a philosopher as a historian.

Becker's attitude toward life and his interest in history were profoundly intellectual. He was actuated by the same lively curiosity that fascinated him as a student of Turner when he daily enjoyed "the inestimable privilege of watching an original and penetrating intelligence at work, playing freely with facts and ideas, handling with discrimination the problems of history, problems which so often turned out to be the problems of life itself." There was in Becker himself this combination of seriousness and play which he here attributes to his teacher, the sense that he was dealing with life itself and yet with the detachment that gives to all purely intellectual activity something of the nature of play. Certainly he conveyed the impression of an original and penetrating intelligence always at work. One wonders whether there was not a trace of autobiography in the fine characterization of Thomas Jefferson which he wrote in his chapter on "The Literary Qualities of the Declaration." Jefferson's peculiar felicity of expression, he says, reflects "a nature exquisitely sensitive, and a mind finely tempered," and these are qualities which Becker shared. Perhaps Becker, like Jefferson and most persons of strongly intellectual bent, lacked "a profoundly emotional apprehension of experience. One might say that Jefferson felt with the mind, as some people think with the heart. He had enthusiasm, but it was enthusiasm engendered by an irrepressible intellectual curiosity." But if there was indeed this lack of emotional apprehension, Becker like Jefferson was saved by "his clear, alert intelligence, his insatiable curiosity, his rarely failing candor, his loyalty to ideas, his humane sympathies."

Becker's historical curiosity apparently carried with it little desire to impart what he found; left to himself he

Introduction

would have been satisfied with the pleasures of the chase. As he said of Turner, "He was caught by his friends and set the task of writing." Fortunately, the charm of his style made him an object of pursuit by friends and publishers. Nearly everything that he published was occasioned by some demand other than the inward urge of the author. His first full-length book, *The Beginnings of the American People* (1915), was part of a publisher's series on American history, as was also *The Eve of the Revolution* (1918). *The United States, an Experiment in Democracy* (1920), was written at the suggestion of Guy Stanton Ford, and *The Declaration of Independence* (1922) at the suggestion of Carl Van Doren, though the manner of its publication was not as originally designed. *The Heavenly City* (1932), which will probably be remembered as Becker's maturest work, was written for the Storrs Lectureship at Yale. It was the first of several series of lectures in his later life: *Progress and Power* (1936) at Stanford; *Modern Democracy* (1940) at the University of Virginia; *Cornell University, Founders and the Founding* (1943) at Cornell; and the present volume at the University of Michigan. His connection with the editorial board of the *Yale Review* accounted for most of his later essays, which were collected, as in *New Liberties for Old* (1941), or expanded, as in *How New Will the Better World Be?* (1944), into book form. Throughout his life personal or professional connections accounted for studies like the essays on "Kansas" and on "Frederick Jackson Turner," or his Presidential Address before the American Historical Association. The labor of writing was for Becker severe, and the facility of his finished work concealed much careful polishing by which that facility was finally achieved. Some kind of special inducement was necessary to make him write at all.

Improperly understood, however, this fact might be quite misleading, for all of Becker's writing grew very naturally

Carl Lotus Becker

out of his own thought and experience. He hated to be bored, and it is quite certain that even the most persuasive publisher could not have made him write on a subject that did not interest him. His published work probably contained less perfunctory writing and reviewing than that of most professional historians. Even at the very beginning, when he was an undergraduate at Wisconsin, it would probably be false to say that Turner influenced him to study the American frontier and its part in creating the American spirit. That interest was native to Becker, and Turner elicited it from Becker's own experience. In *The United States* Becker tells how he had watched the process of Americanizing the German immigrant in the Iowa farming community in which he was born.

> One of my earliest recollections was the appearance in our neighborhood, it must have been about 1878, of a strange family that came to live in the house across the road. To me, a "typical" American boy, they seemed outlandish folk whom one would naturally avoid as suspicious and yet wish to see from some safe point of vantage as a curiosity. The reason for this primitive attitude of mind toward the new-comers was that they were Germans who could barely speak a word or two of English; and a "typical" little American boy, who was himself descended from English, Irish, Dutch, and German ancestors, and whose great-grandfather could not speak English, had never in his life seen nor heard of a German, and now learned for the first time this marvelous thing — namely, that there were people in the world who could not talk as he did, but spoke a kind of gibberish which it was alleged they understood, although no one else did.[2]

From this early experience of the making of Americans, and the consciousness of himself as a "typical" American already made by only one or two generations of the same process, it was but a short step to Turner's generalization about the frontier and the westward movement. It was hardly a longer

[2] *The United States, an Experiment in Democracy* (1920), 240.

Introduction

step from this to the idea of the "American spirit double distilled" which had grown up with the frontier and had been intensified as the wave of settlement moved across the country. Here Becker found the roots of his own belief in democracy and individualism. Given his native interest in ideas and the intellectual side of human behavior, it is easy to see why he turned from the crude activity of the frontier to the more sophisticated expression of American ideas in the Revolution and its most characteristic document. It is easy to see also how his historical work should have culminated in the least provincial expression of the revolutionary philosophy in the French eighteenth century. Here, in the faith of the Enlightenment in intelligence and humanity, in its cool ardor for the rights of man, he found his true intellectual affinity.

In this process Becker had formed also his conception of the aim of historical writing. As the body of human ideas and ideals moves, as it moves forward in space with the frontier or as it moves forward in time, it encounters new conditions and a new environment by which it is continually transformed and to which it must continually adapt itself. If these new conditions are massive and of long duration, as was the case with the American frontier or as was the case when the ideas of medieval Christianity encountered the commercial and the industrial expansion of modern times, they gradually give to the intellectual and the moral ideas of a nation or an age a characteristic pattern. The age comes to have what an artist would call a style, a manner in which its elements cohere and which expresses its typical reaction to the formative forces that have shaped it. The idea in its general outline was far from new, though there is no reason to doubt that Becker formulated it for himself. He might have encountered it in Montesquieu, and possibly the "American spirit" was an echo of the spirit of the laws. Nor was the idea in any way Becker's exclusive property, as a host of books on the modern "mind" or the medieval "mind" bears witness. In any case he made it his own and followed it, long before he seized upon Whitehead's apt phrase, "a climate of opinion," to describe it. The idea defined for him the significant purpose of historical writing. That purpose is the imaginative recapture of a past climate of opinion and its accurate description, first in terms of the powerful forces, social or economic, by which the age is shaped and second in terms of the intellectual and moral and ideal adjustments in which the mind of the age consists. Finally, the human individuals come into the picture as the creators and adapters of ideas, often it must be confessed as somewhat recalcitrant illustrations of the ideas for which they stand. For Becker had no illusions about his methods. He knew that his descriptions ran in terms of abstractions and generalizations which could not even seek to exhaust the embarrassing richness and diversity of human nature.

This conception of what history should attempt went far toward determining the nature of Becker's books, both in their weakness and in their strength. It explains his occasional adventures into what might be called fictional history — "a rather free paraphrase of what some imagined spectator or participant might have thought or said" — in *The Eve of the Revolution* and in the Brookings Lecture on *The Spirit of '76,* which seemed perhaps not quite serious scholarship to his more academic colleagues. For obviously, as Becker himself said, this kind of imaginative recovery cannot be verified by the checking of references. Perhaps there is no strict way in which it can be verified, for verifying a work of art is nonsense. But this kind of writing gave free scope to Becker's sympathetic and imaginative insight into the past and his remarkable sensitivity to currents of thought and feeling. The attempt to recover and describe a past climate of opinion explains very accurately also Becker's conception of style in historical writing. He disliked

Introduction

the notion that writing of any kind, and history in particular, should be dressed up or decorated for the sake of an extraneous effect. Historians who are read for their style, like Bancroft or Gibbon or Macaulay, were for him to that extent bad stylists and bad historians. For if one wishes to describe, the medium should not obscure the thing described. "Only one thing concerns the writer and that is to find an arrangement of words that will fully and exactly convey the thought or feeling which he wishes to convey."

Finally, Becker's conception of what the historian should attempt determined even the structure of his works. His books were invariably short but they were long enough. An appreciative reader will not wish that even a single chapter had been added to *The Heavenly City*. The very perfection with which he did the thing he did was itself a limitation. No one knew this better than Becker, and he accepted the limitation freely as the price to be paid for what he chose to do. The description of the social forces that work within a period and their interplay must run in terms of general notions and abstract concepts that are timeless. The individual and the march of events are unique. The historian must make the two go together, and in the end a solution is impossible, or at least it is a makeshift that can be maintained only in a book of limited extent.

Well, the generalization spreads out in space, but how to get the wretched thing to move forward in time! The generalization, being timeless, will not move forward; and so the harassed historian, compelled to get on with the story, must return in some fashion to the individual, the concrete event, the "thin red line of heroes." Employing these two methods, the humane historian will do his best to prevent them from beating each other to death within the covers of his book. But the strain is great. And while any courageous historian may endure it for one volume, or even for two, few there are who can survive ten.[8]

[8] "Frederick Jackson Turner," *American Masters of Social Science* (1927), 315 f.; reprinted in *Everyman His Own Historian* (1935), 229 f.

Carl Lotus Becker

Becker's view of history was intellectually sophisticated in a high degree. It implied in the historian an extreme form of self-consciousness. The thing that the historian describes is a state of mind induced by a set of conditions which has itself supervened upon an older state of mind. Wherever the historian starts, his material will include the old and the new. It will be a cunning reworking of a tradition already old but now remade in the light of a new human need existent in the historical present. But this is in fact only half the complication, for the historian is himself caught in his own climate of opinion, from which he can no more escape than could the characters in his description. His own writing is part of the process by which his own climate of opinion rewrites the past for a present purpose of which he is the instrument. History seen from Becker's point of view is like a hall of mirrors in which image reflects image until the reality imaged vanishes in a never ending series of images. No point is absolutely fixed, not even that of the historian's own present from which he views the shifting points in his past. Hence it is incumbent on him, more than upon most men, to be aware of his own climate of opinion, since this is the reflecting medium in which he must see whatever past he chooses to describe. This obligation Becker accepted to the full. He sought to re-create imaginatively the social mind that had first produced the democratic tradition, but to do this he had to be aware of the modern mind which in him was attempting to reconstruct this image of a bygone mind. He was a philosopher whose absolute reference points had been caught in a historian's relativism. And his own predicament, as he conceived it, was essentially that which characterizes the modern mind, produced by the dual factors of science and of history itself. In the opening chapter of *The Heavenly City* he describes the modern mind and the impact upon it of science and history, and contrasts it with the medieval mind, formed by theology and logic.

Introduction

Becker was always an omnivorous reader, and his reading bridged the past and the present. In his character as a historian he pursued the sources only so far as suited his purposes. The sources that he used he used meticulously and with a fine historical understanding, but he never acknowledged an obligation to have read all that there was to read. He read more than most historians, however, of the literature of his own day and also of the natural science. This he did in part to gratify an unfailing intellectual curiosity, but in part also to fulfill the historian's obligation to understand himself no less than to understand the past that he describes. Since Becker believed that science is the most powerful formative force in the making of the modern mind, it was inevitable that, within the limits set by his own technical competence, he should have sought continually to understand science, more particularly in its larger significance for present-day ways of thinking, as he sought to understand the repercussion of Newton on the eighteenth century. About the details of scientific discovery, its fact and its gadgets, he cared little. It was the constructive effect of science upon the modern climate of opinion that fascinated him.

One consequence of his thinking on this subject can be briefly described as a complete and unqualified acceptance of scientific naturalism. The world as science reveals it is one that cares nothing for man or for his purposes or his values, a world in which he has emerged by a slow and painful process of evolution from brutality and barbarism and in which ultimately man and all his works are doomed to extinction and nothingness.

Sooner or later there emerges for him [man] the most devastating of all facts, namely, that in an indifferent universe which alone endures, he alone aspires, endeavors to attain, and attains only to be defeated in the end.[4]

---

[4] *Modern Democracy* (1941), 19.

Carl Lotus Becker

Becker's own attitude toward this scientific negation of a religious view of nature seems to have been one of simple acceptance. There is nothing to suggest that it had ever cost him a severe moral struggle, as it had William James, and he was never interested in any philosophical attempt to reconstruct religious belief. Probably he regarded such attempts as out of accord with the temper of modern thought. That the change was intellectually devastating he perceived clearly enough. He could not have failed to see this, considering the care with which he showed that the philosophical framework upon which the eighteenth century had built its democratic ideals depended upon convictions rooted in the Christian Middle Ages and upon Newtonian physics only half understood. He had no doubt that a maturer understanding of science, both its methods and its results, had completely undermined the belief that there is any form of intelligence or purposefulness in the system of nature, except of course as properties of human beings. Becker's belief in the moral worth of the democratic ideal depended therefore upon the possibility of detaching a moral conviction from its traditional religious supports and of retaining it in an intellectual setting that gave it no religious support. Possibly he never fully appreciated the gravity of this problem, but for him it was inevitable and there is little doubt that he regarded it as inevitable for the modern mind.

It was not the tacit naturalism of modern science that affected Becker most intimately. As compared with the absoluteness which the eighteenth century imputed to Newton's laws of nature, it was rather the hypothetical and tentative nature of modern scientific generalization that impressed him. Eighteenth-century science, at least in its own understanding of itself, was still rationalist; its laws were imagined to be eternal truths or necessities of thought justified in the last resort by the impossibility of conceiving the opposite.

Introduction

Modern science is consciously empirical and experimental, and its laws are summations of fact justified only in so far as the event, when they are put to trial, confirms them. The importance of this difference Becker found already emphasized for him by American pragmatism, for he was a constant reader of philosophy as he was of science. In James and Dewey he found the idea that the end and purpose of science is practical control, and from his own reading of history he saw that its outcome is an incredible extension of human power over the forces of nature. This power is purchased precisely at the cost of not asking the old questions about their inner essence. The modern understanding is content with knowing the behavior of things, the manner in which they can be controlled and directed to any desired end — in short, the technique of using them.

So long as we can make efficient use of things, we feel no irresistible need to understand them. No doubt it is for this reason chiefly that the modern mind can be so wonderfully at ease in a mysterious universe.[5]

Science, with its naturalism and pragmatism, was only one of the two great forces which Becker saw at work in the making of the modern mind. The other is history itself, and the effect of history is to reinforce the conclusion already suggested by science. For history reveals the world and human experience as an endless process, without beginning and without end. In it there is nothing permanent and nothing timeless; man and his world are forever in the making. In this Becker found the most powerful solvent for the eternal verities, in morals and in politics, as modern science has found a solvent for the axioms of Newtonian mechanics. For moral truths and ideals also are not axioms but hypotheses, pragmatic factors in the experimental business of living. Becker's book on the United States had as its subtitle "an experiment in democracy." The title had perhaps

[5] *The Heavenly City* (1932), 28.

Carl Lotus Becker

a deeper meaning for Becker than for most of his readers, for in the second edition he reversed title and subtitle, calling the book *Our Great Experiment in Democracy: a History of the United States*. In his preface he explained that he intended to "inject a small question mark" after the assumption that American institutions and American government had "some sacred and sacrosanct quality of the changeless Absolute." Democracy was and remains an experiment, new in its beginning and uncertain in its present, in the face of catastrophic changes in modern economy. "But for the matter of that, what is any human institution, what has it ever been, what can it ever be, but an experiment?" Endless change, endless revision, endless transformation, with at the most only temporary stopping places or relative achievements, were for Becker the lesson of modern history as of modern science. Everything is unstable, he once said, except the idea of instability.

History, however, concerned him far more intimately than science. In science he was, as he well knew, something less than an amateur. It interested him less on its own account than as a force to be reckoned with in assessing its direct effects upon the modern economy and its indirect effects, whether valid or specious, upon the modern mind. History was quite a different matter. It was Becker's life as well as his profession, and he never doubted that the study and writing of history is a work of utmost seriousness. For history as he conceived it is no incidental or extraneous aspect of human experience but something rooted in the nature of consciousness itself. It is therefore in essence not the creation of historians but something which every man must of necessity do for himself, however imperfectly and with whatever mixture of myth and illusion. The historian is important because, by a kind of social division of labor, he does according to a professional standard what the common man is always doing according to the rough and ready standards

Introduction

of his own limited experience. This was the meaning of the title that Becker chose for his Presidential Address before the Historical Association, "Everyman His Own Historian." It was a deeper penetration into philosophy than historians are accustomed to or perhaps would have found palatable had it not been enlightened by Becker's wit and his inimitable style. But from his point of view it was no casual excursion. It summed up not only what he had learned from a lifetime of historical study and writing but also his maturest reflections on the philosophy of the art, or, if one prefers, the science, that he practiced. Essentially there was little in it which might not have been gleaned from the asides and the remarks that he had thrown into his earlier writings, if a reader were penetrating enough to catch the implications of those remarks.

What makes human experience inescapably historical is the fact that the present consciousness of every man is but a point poised between the past and the future. Consciousness is a succession of fleeting presents that are always receding into the past and giving place to a new present. The present is as short as you wish, for it can be divided and subdivided until it vanishes in a point. But what is far more curious is the fact that the present may also be as long as you wish, for men speak of the present moment, the present day, the present year, or the present epoch. What holds the present together with the past is the strange conscious power of memory, and accordingly Becker could say that history, reduced to its lowest terms, is simply "the memory of things said and done." Memory reaches back into the past and pulls together for every man "his little world of endeavor," by co-ordinating the things said and done yesterday with his present perceptions and with the things to be said and done tomorrow. "Without this historical knowledge, this memory of things said and done, his to-day would be aimless and his to-morrow without significance." But equally, the present is held to the future by the no less strange conscious powers of expectation or anticipation, of hope and fear, and memory is no aimless or motiveless recovery of the past but a recovery mainly for the sake of a purpose to be fulfilled in the future. To this present thus united by memory and purpose to the past and the future Becker gives the name, borrowed from William James, of the "specious present." The power of making this union is the peculiar quality of consciousness, and the capacity for having a specious present that can be deliberately and purposefully enlarged and diversified and enriched seemed to Becker to be the peculiar quality of man, the reason why he alone of all animals creates a civilization. Thus understood, history cannot be divorced from life itself.

The theory of mind that Becker thus turned to a better understanding of his own subject had philosophical connections of which he was well aware. It was the conception of consciousness which James had developed in his *Psychology* and which he enlarged in his brilliantly suggestive essays in the eighties and nineties. What it means is that mind — thought, perception, memory, and feeling — is inextricably interwoven with purpose and action; consciousness is "there," as James said, only for the sake of behavior. Its meaning and importance are measured by the degree and the manner in which it affects conduct, or, to put it bluntly, its validity is to be tested by its utility. Far more systematically, and with far more reference to the social questions that interested Becker, James's suggestions were elaborated in the long series of books and essays by which John Dewey made pragmatism the most widely discussed topic in American philosophy. How much of this literature Becker read it is impossible to say. Certainly he cared little for the niceties of philosophical system-making, but he could not fail to be continuously interested in what was so typically the American philosophy of his time. Long before his Presi-

Introduction

dential Address he had made pragmatism in its general idea his own. In an essay that he wrote in 1913, with an academic title not at all like Becker ("Some Aspects of the Influence of Social Problems and Ideas upon the Study and Writing of History" [6]), he said flatly that ideas and beliefs and prepossessions originate in practical interests and "derive validity from the service they render in solving problems which grow out of community life." A bald assertion like this, however, can easily be misleading. It sounds as if Becker were adopting a philosophy when in fact he was merely putting a convenient label on a conclusion of his own. A philosophical doctrine of any kind interested him less on its own account than on account of what he took it to signify. The question he asked about it was not: Is it true? but, as Mill said of Coleridge: What does it mean?

The pragmatic theory that intelligence is interwoven with purpose and behavior attracted Becker because it agreed with his own conclusion about history. It explained why the philosophy and even the science of an age, and in general all its intellectual creations, take on a style that is colored by the social and economic problems of that age. It explained both why there is a climate of opinion for the historian to describe and also why his description must run in terms of interests and prepossessions provided by his own climate of opinion. Historical writing is marked by what Becker, and also some of his critics, called "relativism." By the critics the term was reproachfully intended, but Becker accepted it at its face value. Every historian must of necessity speak from his own specious present. And since consciousness selects its memories in the light of present purposes, the historian like everyone must draw from his documents and sources such facts as appear to him to have a present meaning. Facts are not passively mirrored just as they were, but are selected and interpreted to meet the needs

[6] *American Journal of Sociology,* XVIII (1912–13), 641–75.

of the present, which in turn depend upon the purposes of the future. Hence history must be continually rewritten and brought down to date, even though no new factual information has come to hand, for at least the present purpose of the historian and his society changes from generation to generation. The historian is played upon, as all men are, by the practical interests and the intellectual forces of the age in which he lives. The least he can do with historical facts is to select them and put them into a pattern which appears to him to be important in the light of what he believes will be done or ought to be done. The historian's imagination, when he attempts to re-create a past climate of opinion, is itself controlled and directed by the climate of opinion in which he works.

I mean by relativism no more than that old views are always being displaced by new views, that the facts which historians include or omit, the interconnections between the facts given which they stress, depend in no small part upon the "approach" which seems to them a meaningful one, and that the approach which at any given time will seem significant to the historian depends in no small part upon the social situation in which he finds himself — in short, upon the preconceptions and value judgments, the *Weltanschauung*, of the age in which he lives.[7]

The idea that the intellectual creations of an age reflect its temper and practical interests was continually used by Becker to classify and criticize historical writing. The philosophers of the Enlightenment had sought to reform and reconstruct society in the light of what they believed to be manifest principles of justice and right. For them history was "philosophy teaching by example," and they sought in it for the lessons that might enable them to restore to men their just and natural liberties and to avoid or destroy the tyrannical invasions of liberty. Conceiving that the just and right could be made clear by discovering what was nat-

[7] *Philosophical Review*, XLIX (1940), 363.

Introduction

ural or essential to men, they looked in history for a core of human nature that might be regarded as the same everywhere and always. After the French Revolution had overturned and destroyed legitimate governments and constitutional traditions over most of continental Europe the temper of the time changed and with it the temper of the historians. In the nineteenth century it became the fashion to attribute the destructive upheaval of the Revolution to the illusion, as it then seemed, that men could remake society according to their own fancies. The post-revolutionary historians, especially in Germany, came to stress historical continuity and the growth or development of the nation. Man, as Becker said, was safely imprisoned in society. Nation was conceived to succeed nation according to divine plan, or according to the internal development of the Hegelian Idea — the choice of terms made little difference in Becker's estimation. Natural rights gave place to historic rights, and the interest in constitutional history reflected an almost universal need for rebuilding the political structure of every European government. Responding to the temper of an anti-revolutionary age, the temper of the belief in historical continuity was in general conservative and nationalist, as the temper of the belief in the rights of man had been radical and cosmopolitan. In either case Becker's point was that history was interpreted in the patterns to which the prevailing climate of opinion gave significance.

The sharpest shafts of Becker's wit, however, were reserved for so-called objective history, or history for its own sake, against which his own historical writing was a conscious reaction. Such history seemed to him little better than a form of the literature of escape. It corresponded in his estimation to a decline of nationalism from the stage of idealism, in which it had been imagined as the march of God in the world, to a sordid scramble for power and markets and raw materials. The historian disclaimed moral responsibility because his subject no longer enlisted a moral sympathy that he could avow. But in Becker's opinion the disclaimer was largely self-deception, and the notion of history which it produced was illusory. The idea that facts could be made "to speak for themselves," that history could be made scientific by techniques for criticizing documents or by the mere suppression of the historian's more obvious social interests and judgments of value, was contrary to Becker's reading of both philosophy and history. It neglected the psychological relation of emotion to thought, and also the fact that every historian, even the most scientific, is bound to have some kind of preferences which must manifest themselves in his selection and explanation of facts. It is not, he said, the undiscriminated fact that speaks but the perceiving mind of the historian, prompting the fact according to his own judgment of what it ought to say. What passed current as historical detachment seemed to Becker superficial; he described it derisively as "a set of artificially induced and cultivated repressions such as would enable a careful historian to write . . . an account of the Battle of Cold Harbor without revealing that his father was an ardent admirer of Grant." This kind of detachment is not hard to attain, but it does nothing to insure that the historian will have anything of significance to say.

Objective history in Becker's judgment is really condemned by the fact that it runs the risk of being trivial history. Of it he said in his Presidential Address:

Hoping to find something without looking for it, expecting to obtain final answers to life's riddle by resolutely refusing to ask questions — it was surely the most romantic species of realism yet invented, the oddest attempt ever made to get something for nothing! [8]

[8] "Everyman His Own Historian," *American Historical Review*, XXXVII (1932), 233; reprinted in *Everyman His Own Historian* (1935), 250.

Introduction

Historical detachment as commonly understood Becker described, with more sharpness than his criticism usually displayed, as pernicious because it is "the best substitute for ideas yet invented." Without ideas, and among ideas Becker was convinced that some sort of preferences and moral preconceptions and values must be included, what the historian has to say becomes insignificant, a species of antiquarianism in which, to be sure, ideas of a kind are not avoided but are merely academic and unimportant for any live social interest. Like Charles Beard and other critics of objective history, Becker believed that real historical detachment is produced not by a vain effort to have no interests or prepossessions but by becoming as fully aware as possible of the prepossessions one has. Given intellectual integrity and a consuming intellectual curiosity about the matter to be explained, malicious invention and dishonest selection and distortion are ruled out, because an honest aspiration cannot safely be based upon fabrication. For the rest, as Becker believed, the historian must depend upon a conscious facing of present problems and an explicit awareness of future prospects and ideals. In his literary style this pursuit of self-consciousness was reflected in his habitual use of irony. The ironical description of a prepossession was a vivid way of making his reader realize that a prepossession was there and was affecting the conclusion. Similarly, consciousness of a historian's preconception and of the place of that preconception in the age in which he wrote seemed to Becker the true function of historical criticism. But the critic's own philosophy is an unavoidable factor in his estimate. In a report which he once wrote for the Historical Association on the reviewing of historical books, Becker said: "In seeking to avoid having a philosophy of history, the historian does not succeed in not having one; perhaps after all he succeeds only in having a bad one."

Becker's serious quarrel with objective history was not

due to the badness of its philosophy, a fault that he would readily have forgiven if he had found it otherwise enlightening. His final objection was that the historian's avoidance of philosophical and practical commitments was dereliction from his high calling. History for its own sake can never be serious history, just as art for art's sake is the formula not of great art but of æstheticism. Great history is the product of social crisis, an unavoidable aspect of intelligent social action because it is one means by which an age becomes conscious of what it is doing, in the light of what it has done and what it hopes to do. This belief on Becker's part, for which pragmatism gave him a philosophical formula, was indeed the lesson he had learned from Turner, that history is of a piece with life itself. The key to American history is not the continuity of its institutions with those of Europe from which they came but the transformation of those institutions by the problems set in a new environment, especially of course the frontier. With S. R. Gardiner's dictum that "comparison of the past with the present is altogether destructive of real historical knowledge" Becker contrasted the assertion of Turner that "a just public opinion and a statesmanlike treatment of present problems demand that they be seen in their historical relations, in order that history may hold the lamp for conservative reform." The belief that history may hold the lamp for reform, and must in any case hold the lamp for some kind of change, was an aspect of Becker's deep intellectual affinity with the eighteenth century. He hoped, and on occasion he believed, that the swing of American philosophy away from romanticism and Hegelianism had brought it closer to its point of origin, and the reaction against objective history had for him a similar meaning. This was the reason for his sympathetic reception of the "new history" of James Harvey Robinson and H. G. Wells. When he was in an optimistic mood, such as that perhaps produced in him by the Progressive cam-

Introduction

paign of 1912, he could hail this change as symbolizing "the arising of a new faith, born of science and democracy" — "the belief that society can, by taking thought, modify the conditions of life, and thereby indefinitely improve the happiness and welfare of all men."

This change in history and philosophy, therefore, which Becker sometimes called relativism and which he often identified with pragmatism, implied for him two things. On its negative side it was a renunciation of the arrogance and sterility, as it seemed to him, of the claim that historians are detached observers of the human scene, able like gods to see the past "as it really was." On its positive side it was a deep conviction of the importance of the historian's work as part of the continual change that is going on in society, and ideally as part of an intelligent effort to reconstruct society in the light of humane and democratic ends. The historical imagination is not a mirroring of the past but a reformulation of it in the interest of present needs and future purposes; once this is admitted, the historian may possibly make his art a factor in a planned and directed reconstruction of society for human welfare. In his Presidential Address Becker summarized his views of the historian's work in his own inimitable fashion as follows:

> It should be a relief to us to renounce omniscience, to recognize that every generation, our own included, will, must inevitably, understand the past and anticipate the future in the light of its own restricted experience, must inevitably play on the dead whatever tricks it finds necessary for its own peace of mind. The appropriate trick for any age is not a malicious invention designed to take anyone in, but an unconscious and necessary effort on the part of "society" to understand what it is doing in the light of what it has done and what it hopes to do.[9]

It is not surprising that passages like this — and they could be multiplied in large number — surprised or even

[9] "Everyman His Own Historian," loc. cit., XXXVII (1932), 235; reprinted in *Everyman His Own Historian* (1935), 253.

shocked some of Becker's colleagues. The description of history as a trick played on the dead — a favorite witticism which he borrowed from Voltaire — was certainly provocative language and intentionally so, for Becker was always "injecting small question marks" after the supposed certainties of both scholarship and popular belief. Certainly also the assertion that the trick was played for the sake of peace of mind might suggest that the desire for a comfortable conclusion carried more weight than an honest assessment of the difficulties and the search for a sound and tenable solution. All this need not be taken too seriously, since it was not seriously meant. The interesting part of the quotation is rather the contrast between its first and its second sentence. History, to be sure, is a trick, since it cannot reproduce the past as it was, or even as the dead experienced it when they were alive. But there are, it appears, tricks and tricks. Some are malicious and some are appropriate parts of an effort to understand. But can the historian or anyone else tell which is which? Malice indeed might be detected as a moral defect in the historian, but even if he were malicious, it would not follow that what he said was untrue. And certainly Becker was not simple-minded enough to think that non-malicious historians always tell the truth or even say anything worth listening to. In any case what the historian says is an invention, even if it is a part of the necessary effort to understand. In short, if historical interpretation is an imaginative construction, how are good inventions to be distinguished from bad?

This question, posed by Becker but not answered in the Presidential Address, was indeed not one of his own making. It was deeply involved in the social philosophy of the age whose insights and whose puzzlements he reflected so accurately. With better fortune he might never have had to face it, but neither Becker nor his age was fortunate. The question may be stated thus: just what sort of thing does

Introduction

the social mind invent when it is confronted with the decay of its institutions and the breaking down of its settled habits and inherited convictions? Consciousness is *there,* as James had said, for the sake of will and action, and it must satisfy the need for peace of mind, for whole-souled and unimpeded activity. But what does consciousness supply? Two contrary answers run through the social philosophy of the later nineteenth and twentieth century. The one conceives of mind as engaged in finding reasonable solutions to social problems, solutions that conserve and realize the values inherent in the past and move into the future along a line of moral progress. According to this understanding of pragmatic philosophy, a new faith in science and democracy, as Becker had paraphrased it, is to improve indefinitely the happiness and welfare of all men. Such in general was the hope, so congenial to American optimism, held out by the pragmatism of John Dewey. Unfortunately, quite a different answer was possible and was often given, for American pragmatism was only one way of reading the general thesis that thought is intermeshed in feeling and will. Faced with the shipwreck of its hopes, the mind can, and often does, seek its peace in the making of myths and illusions, as Becker himself said, "by creating ideal worlds of semblance, Utopias of other time and place." Here it may shelter itself in a quietist's dream, but equally its dream may be violent and world-shaking, issuing out in revolutionary action prompted by its own apocalyptic visions and the need to assert its own fanatical will. Such was the view of the mind's inventive power suggested by Schopenhauer and more radically affirmed by Nietzsche. In his later life Becker came to see this way of subordinating intelligence to will as the philosophical foundation of fascism and the fruitful mother of social barbarism. The contrast is indeed striking. According to the one view social values evolve in an orderly and intelligent way along with the means of realizing them, and the standards of intellectual validity and integrity guarantee the soundness of both ends and means. About the fundamental values inherent in human welfare there is assumed to be a working agreement among all men of good will. According to the other view social change is discontinuous and revolutionary. Its motive power is a Promethean will bent upon bringing down fire from heaven, a will which has no measure except the strength of its own desire, and its values are myths created to fortify its own fanatical self-assertion.

As between these two views of the inventive power of the mind and the manner of its relation to will and action, thus set down in naked contrariety, Becker knew perfectly which he must choose. His conscious affinity for the eighteenth century was due to an instinctive belief that social intelligence, issuing in the twin faiths of science and democracy, is the root of all the solid achievements of civilization. Yet there was perhaps something a shade paradoxical in his preference for the cool ardors of the philosophers who preceded a revolution and his distrust of the violent emotions without which revolutions cannot be made. Becker wrote about the eve of two revolutions, but never about a revolution. It was the Heavenly City and not the Terror that enlisted his sympathy. But how could he be certain that human ingenuity extended to having one without the other, or that Diderot represented the meaning of the rights of man better than Robespierre? So long as it was merely a question of writing history, the historian no doubt might begin and end where he pleased. In real life revolutions run their course without regard for historians' preferences. And it was Becker's fate, and the fate of his generation, to witness a revolution of which Nietzsche was a better exponent than John Dewey.

Perhaps there was a paradox too behind Becker's confidence, and the confidence of American pragmatism, that science and democracy remain twin faiths for the modern

Introduction

mind. Becker's analysis of the philosophy behind the Declaration of Independence and the French Enlightenment had demonstrated that the faith in reason and nature had its roots far back in the ethical tradition of Christianity. Temporarily it had construed science as a support for its faith in reason and nature, but Becker was clear that such a construction was not tenable in the light of the maturer development of science itself. The belief in natural and inalienable human rights he had described as "a humane and engaging faith," but it was still a faith. To ask whether it was true or false, he had said, was "essentially a meaningless question," because its premises to the modern mind had become simply irrelevant. Liberal democracy, as it turned out, like communism and fascism, was an ideology — that faintly disdainful word, suggesting both myth and aspiration, with which the period between the Wars liked to describe social ideals in the mass. Meanwhile science as it advanced separated itself more and more from pronouncements about the value of any human achievement or the intrinsic rightness of any course of action. It brought to men a wonderful access of power over things and indeed over other men, but its recipes for control could be used indifferently for any end whatever whether good or bad, and the farther it went, the less it seemed to have to say about any distinction between good and bad. The chasm between moral ideals and matter-of-fact knowledge became deeper and broader, for Becker knew well that ideologies consist in moral judgments and not in scientifically verifiable propositions. Science and democracy seemed to have no logical relationship to each other. Though the modern mind might be shaped by science, it was hard to see a reason why it must equally be turned toward democracy.

A paradox is not fatal to philosophy, but changing times can make a paradox acute. Without the crisis of the thirties Becker's paradox need never have troubled him. For democracy, despite its failures and the inevitable discrepancies between the ideal and the realization, had, for more than a century, seemed in a fair way to ultimate success. At all events, its fundamental values, both moral and political — civil liberty, constitutional representative government, freedom of thought and discussion, the worth of individual personality — had suffered no frontal attack and had met with no determined denial. Then came the frankly undemocratic philosophies of communism and fascism, the fall of free government, such as it had been, in Italy, the greater fall in Germany, and the success of dictatorship in Russia, all involved with a world-wide depression that shook democracy even in the free countries. Worse followed bad in the futility of democratic diplomacy, the outbreak of the Great War, the successes of Germany, the collapse of France, and the weakness and indecisiveness of American public opinion. With characteristic sensitiveness Becker's thought and feeling followed them all, reflecting the shifting temper of the time, first the pessimism about democracy in the thirties, later the revival and reassertion of a democratic faith in the forties. The last was largely a return to the mood of qualified confidence characteristic of him before the crisis.

It was not the case, of course, that Becker had ever been an unqualified or an uncritical admirer of democracy. From the end of the first World War, possibly from the Progressive campaign of 1912, he had believed that democracy, whatever its political success, was a failure in its traditional economic program. Freedom of speech and thought was one thing; freedom of business enterprise was another. He had closed his study of the American experiment with these words:

The time for national complacency is past. The sentimentalism that turns away from facts to feed on platitudes, the provincialism which fears ideas and plays at politics in the spirit

Introduction

of the gambler or the amateur, will no longer serve. The time has come when the people of the United States must bring all their intelligence and all their idealism to the consideration of the subtler realities of human relations, as they have formerly to the much simpler realities of material existence: this at least they must do if America is to be in the future what it has been in the past — a fruitful experiment in democracy.[10]

From this conclusion, once formed, he never departed. In 1944 he said flatly that some form of economic collectivism is inevitable; the only choice is whether it shall be communism or fascism or some form of modernized liberal democracy. Domestic as well as international problems he regarded as basically economic, and he was quite aware that for a century the tendency, in Europe and in the United States and under all forms of government, had been toward an extension of the regulation of business by government. He looked for no reversal of that direction. An international political settlement, however excellent, he said, will not end the present era of war and aggression because political conflict and confusion in the modern world are the results of an underlying economic confusion and conflict. The fundamental problems of the day — the antagonism of social classes at home and the conflict of nations abroad — all presuppose, as Becker always believed, the political regulation of economic relationships. The question is whether the necessary regulation can take place by democratic means within a society that still preserves the democratic civil liberties.

The defects of democracy are one thing and its irrevocable breakdown is quite another, and it was the possibility of the latter that was posed by the events of the thirties. Theoretically this was quite within the gamut of Becker's philosophy. If endless change is the law of history, there is no reason why the ideals of democracy should be permanent. There is always the possibility that democracy is a

[10] *The United States, an Experiment in Democracy* (1920), 333.

Carl Lotus Becker

passing phase, a way-station on the road of human progress, destined like so many others to be by-passed when it has served its turn. Whatever the value of its ultimate ideals, its successful working is dependent upon certain material conditions which democracy did not create and cannot restore if they are once irretrievably lost. This conclusion had been implicit in Becker's philosophy from the start, but the failure of the Weimar Republic made him more keenly aware of it. Surveying history in the large, he was constrained to admit that democracy is a new-comer in the moral world; for untold centuries men had lived mostly by instinct and with only a modicum of intelligence, and the rights of the individual are chiefly conspicuous by their absence. Where they have been recognized and established, this has been chiefly in small countries and for brief times in which a relatively high degree of economic security could be taken for granted. Social problems can be settled by discussion only if the diversity of interests is not too great and the problems are not too complex. The party system, inseparable from any democratic machinery of government, works best when the losing side in a controversy need not surrender what it regards as its vital interests, because the common interest is generally understood and generally conceded to overrule all special interests. In short, government by discussion works best, as Becker said in 1939, "when there is nothing of profound importance to discuss, and when there is plenty of time to discuss it. . . ." Possibly his pessimism about the possibilities of democracy touched bottom when he wrote in 1932, under the stress of the great depression:

Choose as we will or can, the event is less likely to be decided by our choices than by the dumb pressure of common men and machines. The intellectual liberty we so highly prize is of little moment to the average man, since he rarely uses it, while the liberties he can make use of are just now of diminishing value

Introduction

to him. Of the many liberties which, in our free democratic society, the average man now enjoys (if that is the word), I will mention the one which concerns him most. He is free to take any job that offers, if any offers; if none offers, free to look for one that will pay a bare living wage, or less: if none is found, free to stand in line begging a crust from charity, or from the government that makes him a free man. What the average man wants, more than he wants this kind of liberty, is security; and when the pressure of adverse circumstances becomes adequate he will support those who can and will give it to him.[11]

It makes a curious contrast to set side by side with this a quotation from Somerset Maugham with which Becker ended an article in 1944 and which he used also when he expanded two or three of his essays into the book entitled *How New Will the Better World Be?*

If a nation values anything more than freedom, it will lose its freedom; and the irony of it is that if it is comfort or money that it values more, it will lose that too.

But in the later thirties and early forties events crowded Becker close, as they did the whole democratic society for which he spoke. He came to see, as who of us did not, that the issue involved more than economic insecurity or the discrepancies between democratic ideals and their inadequate realization in democratic institutions and democratic societies. The devastation of Poland and the downfall of France posed the question whether the humane ideals inherent in the democratic tradition, or even the decencies of civilized society, could survive in a world in which dictatorship had chosen to rest its case on the arbitrament of naked force. The change in Becker's manner of writing about democracy appeared dramatically in the juxtaposition of two essays, one written in 1939 entitled "When Democratic Virtues Disintegrate," the other written in 1940 entitled "Some Generalities That Still Glitter," which were

---

[11] "Liberalism — a Way Station," *The Saturday Review of Literature*, December 3, 1932; reprinted in *Everyman His Own Historian* (1935), 98 f.

republished side by side in the book *New Liberties for Old.* In the first he was still thinking in terms of the contrast between democratic liberties in the civil and political spheres and what he had long regarded as the false or negative liberty of economic *laissez faire.* "Freedom of the individual in the economic realm has in fact come to mean economic subjection for the many and freedom only for the few." In the second he turned sharply upon "a certain insensitiveness to the moral implications of conduct which characterizes the modern temper" and which he traced to the anti-intellectualism or relativism or activism of modern thought, issuing at its crudest in the doctrine of Thrasymachus in Plato's *Republic* that "Might makes right; justice is the interest of the stronger." Becker's pragmatism, like that of William James and John Dewey, had always taken for granted — whether it accounted for them or not — the moral certainty of good faith, integrity, humanity, and respect for human personality which, as he had argued in *The Heavenly City,* made democracy continuous with the tradition of Christian civilization. No more than James had he identified utility with a worship of "the bitch goddess success."

From this point on, the main theme of Becker's essays became an explicit and conscious reaffirmation of these moral values. The incredible sophistries of fascism in argument, its cynical disavowal of integrity and good faith in political dealings, and its conscious adoption of cruelty and terrorism in action revolted every fiber of Becker's moral being. What he feared even more — and in this again he reflected a common reaction of the day — was the faltering and flaccid reaction of public opinion in the democracies to these sophistries and barbarities, the willingness to sacrifice even moral ideals in order to avoid war, and the tendency to pitch public discussion at the intellectual and moral level of the "hard-boiled" and the "wise guy." With his native intellectual curiosity, Becker had been willing to ex-

Introduction

plore the ideologies of communism and fascism, to set them beside the ideology of liberal democracy, even to assess at its highest the discrepancies between democratic ideals and practice. But after the fall of France the issue was no longer philosophy; it was war. If this involved some inconsistency with what he had elsewhere said about the relativity of moral values to social circumstances — and Becker was aware that such a charge might be made — he accepted the possibility cheerfully, for minor inconsistencies did not bother him. A difference of emphasis he was ready to admit, but nothing more, for he knew that he had always believed profoundly in the democratic virtues, even when he was engaged in injecting a small question mark after their absoluteness. In the bottom of his heart he had always believed, as he said in 1915 and as he was to say again in 1940, that the democratic values were "basic truths which no criticism can seriously impair," whatever their philosophical basis or lack of it.

I should like to believe that the essays as a whole are essentially consistent in the premises they start from and the general conclusions they point to. If they are, it is because premises and conclusions derive in the last analysis from certain convictions I entertain — prejudices, if you prefer — prejudgments as to the essential values of life. I believe, without being able to prove but equally without being able to doubt, that the primary values of life, upon which in the long run all other values depend, are intelligence, integrity, and good will. Taken separately, any one of these may avail little. Good will, apart from intelligence and integrity, may be a futile or even a vicious thing. Intelligence leads to knowledge, and knowledge confers power, enabling men to transform instead of endlessly to repeat their activities. But knowledge and the power it confers may be used either to degrade or to ennoble the life of man. Only when guided and restrained by good will and integrity can they be used effectively to achieve the good life.[12]

[12] *New Liberties for Old* (1941), xvi f.

Carl Lotus Becker

The emphasis of Becker's last essays is upon the achievements of democracy rather than upon its shortcomings. Hitler and Stalin, he said, "have revealed to us the advantages of democratic institutions and the reality of the humane values that are traditionally associated with them," though he admitted ruefully that Hitler and Stalin were an exorbitant price to pay for a little wisdom. In these essays he tried to ward off in anticipation the reaction which he knew must come with the close of the War. He distrusted alike the moods of exaltation and of depression which arise out of the characteristic sentimentality of American political thought. The generous but ignorant and provincial enthusiasm of the war waged to make the world safe for democracy had ended in the disillusionments of the return to "normalcy," which was equally ignorant and provincial without being generous. Becker dreaded seeing a like reaction of weariness from the exaltation of the present war. War, as he knew, creates more problems than it solves, and of social and political problems he had often said that they are not solved but transformed. The new world, he urged, which was to follow the defeat of Germany, would not be very new, and only by long sustained and intelligent effort could it be made a little better. The sentiment of nationalism and the drive toward imperialism would emerge stronger rather than weaker, and indeed it was the nationalism of the occupied countries that in the end would defeat Germany, as it was the cohesiveness of British imperialism that for a year had stood alone against her after Dunkerque. The notion that some panacea could make politics cease to depend on force now seemed to Becker a fantastic and dangerous illusion which could end only in disillusionment. With all his power he urged the advantages of a piecemeal attack upon limited problems, in international as well as domestic politics, rather than a trust in grandiose schemes of reconstruction. The way of intelligence is neither real-

Introduction

ism nor idealism, but a clear-sighted grasp of realities patiently controlled in the interest of attainable ideals.

Yet in Becker's last essays there was a note of restrained exaltation, not new exactly, but clearer and more explicit, because after the moral and intellectual confusions of the interwar period it was possible again, as he said, to refer to the Declaration of Independence without apology. In some sense the rights of man had always been for Becker, if not moral absolutes in a cosmic sense, at least the relative absolutes of any truly civilized society. For him as for the Age of Reason intelligence overlapped both the achievements of knowledge and the achievements of moral progress, and in some way which he never professed to understand truth and goodness were inseparably joined. Faith in the ideals of democracy was of a piece with a larger faith, unfolding perhaps through the ages but certainly contained in the moral insight of the saints and sages, which was the clue to all that made life worth living.

To have faith in the dignity and worth of the individual man as an end in himself, to believe that it is better to be governed by persuasion than by coercion, to believe that fraternal good will is more worthy than a selfish and contentious spirit, to believe that in the long run all values are inseparable from the love of truth and the distinterested search for it, to believe that knowledge and the power it confers should be used to promote the welfare and happiness of all men rather than to serve the interests of those individuals and classes whom fortune and intelligence endow with temporary advantage — these are the values which are affirmed by the traditional democratic ideology. But they are older and more universal than democracy and do not depend upon it. They have a life of their own apart from any particular social system or type of civilization. They are the values which, since the time of Buddha and Confucius, Solomon and Zoroaster, Plato and Aristotle, Socrates and Jesus, men have commonly employed to measure the advance or the decline of civilization, the values they have celebrated in the saints and sages whom they have agreed to canonize. They are the values that readily lend themselves to rational justification, yet need no justification.[13]

Becker fulfilled in his life and writing his own ideal of the high calling of the historian — to reflect on things said and done in the past of mankind, to see the past as it lives on into the present, to clarify and express for the present those generous impulses which it hopes to achieve in the future. By this work of self-consciousness the generous impulse is transformed into an abiding ideal, never to be realized perhaps in its entirety but giving meaning and direction to human effort. Like a finely sensitized plate Becker's mind caught and recorded the thought and the feeling of his time, sometimes its temporary and passing phases but more generally its deeper and more lasting aspirations. Sharing profoundly the American faith in liberty and equality which had been the guiding light of the Founding Fathers and of the American frontier, he had plumbed the forces, intellectual and social, which had disintegrated the framework of abstract ideas in which that faith had traditionally been enshrined. With complete intellectual honesty he faced the negations which science and criticism and an industrialized economy had brought upon the theology, or the thinly veiled theological philosophy, that the Fathers had imagined to be the immovable foundation of a democratic faith. From the negations he sought to disentangle the more lasting moral affirmations which, in the future as in the past, might still enlighten the struggle for a civilization devoted to democratic ends. In this task there could be for Becker no illusion of permanence. Of him must be said what he said of other historians:

> For my part I do not ask of any historian more than this, that he should have exerted in his generation a notable influence upon many scholars in many branches of humanistic study.[14]

[13] *New Liberties for Old* (1941), 149 f.
[14] "Frederick Jackson Turner," *American Masters of Social Science* (1927), 317; reprinted in *Everyman His Own Historian* (1935), 231.

Introduction

Such influence he did exert, but not upon scholars or study alone, for, as Becker believed, scholars and study are incidents in the adventure of living and in the greater society of which scholars are a part. For the democracy of his time Becker posed the greater problem — perhaps the final problem of emancipated intelligence: an idealism without illusions and a realism without cynicism.

GEORGE H. SABINE

Ithaca, New York
June 22, 1945.

Freedom and Responsibility in the American Way of Life

I

The American Political Tradition

Liberty consists in the power to do whatever does not injure others.

Declaration of the Rights of Man

WHEN I had the signal honor of being invited to give these lectures I was informed that the terms of Mr. Cook's bequest permitted me to choose any subject within the general field of "American institutions and their preservation." This opened to me a sufficiently wide field, but it seemed to me that the first series of lectures, instead of dealing with any particular American institution, might properly be devoted to those broad general rights or freedoms upon which our system of government rests, and which, according to the Declaration of Independence, all just governments exist to secure. This subject seemed all the more appropriate in view of the fact that for some years now half the world has been engaged in the desperate task of combating an alien system that in theory denies, and in practice would destroy, all of the rights and freedoms which are essential, not only to the democratic way of life, but to any way of life that can rightly be called civilized. It seemed, therefore, both timely in itself and suited to this occasion to devote these lectures to the general subject of Freedom and Responsibility in the American Way of Life.

But, it may be asked, why not confine the discussion to Freedom in the American Way of Life? "Freedom" is an at-

Freedom and Responsibility

tractive word, and freedom itself is a fine thing. We all love our freedoms. Why, then, inject into the discussion the tiresome word "responsibility"? No doubt some people welcome responsibility, but most of us would perhaps just as soon not be burdened with it. In any case, our rights and freedoms are enumerated in the Federal and state constitutions, but do the constitutions enumerate our duties and responsibilities? Well, there is, to be sure, no Bill of Responsibilities in our constitutions, but a careful reading of them will disclose the annoying fact that for every right or freedom that they confer they impose, implicitly if not explicitly, a corresponding obligation or responsibility.

Two examples will suffice to make this clear. The Connecticut Constitution of 1818 contains this statement: "Every citizen may freely speak, write, and publish his sentiments on all subjects, being responsible for the abuse of that liberty." Here a freedom is defined and conferred — freedom of speech and of the press; but it is conjoined with a responsibility — responsibility for the abuse of that freedom. Again, the Federal Constitution contains this statement: "Treason against the United States, shall consist only in levying war against them, or adhering to their enemies, giving them aid and comfort. No person shall be convicted of treason, unless on the testimony of two witnesses to the same overt act, or on confession in open court." Here an obligation is imposed — the obligation to be loyal to the United States; but it is conjoined with a right — the right of not being punished for disloyalty except in a court of law and on specific evidence. If, then, we examine our constitutions looking for our rights, we shall find them; but we shall also find, in the case of each right, some responsibility inconveniently intruding to limit it.

I have therefore united freedom and responsibility in this discussion because they are united in our constitutions and laws; but also for another and more fundamental reason — because the nature of freedom and responsibility is such that they cannot be discussed, still less dealt with, to any good purpose separately. Freedom unrestrained by responsibility becomes mere license; responsibility unchecked by freedom becomes mere arbitrary power. The question, then, is not whether freedom and responsibility shall be united, but how they can be united and reconciled to the best advantage. This is indeed the central problem of all political philosophy and practice, the problem of the one and the many — the difficulty being to reconcile the desirable liberties of the individual with the necessary power of government in such a way as to do justice as well as may be to the desires and the interests of all individuals and classes in society.

There is, needless to say, no universally valid rule for solving this fundamental problem; or rather, the only universally valid rule does not help us much in solving it in particular cases. "Liberty," says the French Declaration of the Rights of Man and the Citizen, "consists in the power to do whatever does not injure others." Very true. But the essential question, always difficult and sometimes impossible to answer, is: What action by what person or persons under what specific circumstances does injure others, or so far and so persistently injure others that it needs to be restricted or forbidden? Liberty is a variable thing, appearing in different guises at different times and to different people. One man's liberty may easily be another man's bondage. The French nobles in the eighteenth century spoke of their liberties, but for the French peasants these liberties were oppressions, and to us they have all the appearance of unjust privileges. For the owners of English cotton mills in the 1830's freedom of contract was a cherished liberty, but for the anemic women and children who contracted to work in the mills because the alternative was starvation, it was a species of wage slavery. Freedom of the press is a valuable liberty to those who publish books and newspapers, but it has by no means the same value to those who rarely take their pen in hand and find it rather heavier than the sword when they do. Freedom of speech is a capital asset to the vendors of patent medicines and the corporations offering air-blown stocks to the public, but such vendors and corporations have at different times been so far unable to distinguish freedom of speech from freedom of lying that their freedom had to be curbed.

Liberty is likewise differently regarded by different nations. The pre-Hitler Germans were free to do many things, but they were content, indeed happy, to have many actions *verboten* that we think harmless and even desirable; and, whereas we are apt to think the Russians enslaved, the Russians themselves appear to feel that they are freer than we are. Not long since, a Russian scholar said to me that the liberties that Americans prize so highly seem to the Russians too negative to be of much use. "Your American freedoms," he said, "are mostly *freedoms from something,* whereas the Russian freedoms are *freedoms to do something.*" The distinction seemed to me a superficial one, since any liberty to do something implies a freedom from interference with that doing, and any freedom from something implies a liberty to do what the doer might otherwise be prevented from doing. But what my Russian acquaintance meant, I suppose, is that the freedoms enumerated in our constitutions are mostly defined as freedoms from governmental interference with the activities of the individual, so that the American form of government guarantees the freedom of the individual, as one may say, by letting him alone; whereas in Russia the government guarantees the freedom of the individual, not by letting him alone, but by seeing to it that he has a job, a place to live, an education, medical care, and other similar good things. "The real difference," my Russian acquaintance said, "is that in Russia we regard the government as our friend, whereas you Americans seem to feel that the government is your enemy."

There is some truth in this distinction; enough at all events to bring us within sight of the characteristic attitude of the people of the United States towards the function of government and the liberties of the citizen. We do not regard the government as an enemy exactly, but rather, let us say, as a friendly enemy, a neighbor who will probably do well enough if you keep your eye on him. Certainly for us the state is not the abstract mystical blind Moloch of German philosophy, made tangible and active in a government that must be looked up to with awe and reverence or worshiped as something semidivine. For us, state and government are one thing, and that thing merely a number of men whom we choose as our agents to do for us certain necessary and prosaic things. We choose them and hope for the best, but we limit their terms of office and always reserve the right to turn the rascals out for good reasons, or even for no reason at all, if we feel like it. No, we do not regard the government as an enemy; but for all that we more or less agree with Thomas Paine, who said that whereas society springs from men's virtues, government springs from their vices, and is therefore a necessary evil. Our characteristic and traditional attitude is to view with alarm any new and unusual activity on the part of the government, and to point with pride to the new and unusual things that the people have done, and will always do on their own initiative if the government only refrains from undue meddling and minds its own business.

The explanation of this traditional attitude towards the function of government and the liberty of the citizen is not to be found in any inherent virtues or defects of the Americans themselves. It is to be found, first, in the circumstances of their history, which have enabled them, until comparatively recent times at least, to get on very well with a mini-

Freedom and Responsibility

mum of governmental regulation; and, secondly, in their traditional democratic political philosophy, which, as formulated in the eighteenth century, was based on the assumption, among others, that the best form of government is the one that governs least. What, then, were these peculiar circumstances of American history, and how was this historical experience rationalized in the traditional democratic political philosophy?

2

On certain conventional occasions we rise and sing to the land of the free and the home of the brave, land of the Pilgrim's pride, land where our fathers died. No doubt there is as much symbolic truth in these phrases as one can reasonably expect to find in a patriotic hymn. But it is worth noting that in all the stages of our history our fathers, if we go back a few generations, mostly died somewhere else. We are a collection of people from all the nations of Europe, and even of the world — people who have in successive generations come here in order to escape oppression or to improve the material conditions of life. Goethe expressed this general feeling when he exclaimed: "America, you have it better!" I once asked a Greek who had recently come to this country how he liked it here. He agreed with Goethe. "I like it fine," he said. "I am a Greek Jew. So what? No one asks am I a Greek Jew. In America is everything better for poor people like me." This is the essential fact: in America everything has always been better for poor people. It is this conviction, no doubt, that makes us a united nation, although by all the rules known to an Adolf Hitler we should be neither united nor a nation. Native- and foreign-born alike are united by the profound conviction that America has the best of it. We are attached to the U. S. A. less for what it is than for what it has to offer, less because of its sacred rills and templed hills than because it is the place in the world where all comers can find the best opportunity to do what they like and get what they want. In this sense it has always been, and has always been thought by the peoples of Europe to be, the land of the free because it is the land of opportunity.

It was in this light — a somewhat too glamorous light, no doubt — that the first settlers looked to the new world of America. John Winthrop tells us that he and his associates decided to remove from England for two reasons mainly. One was that they wished to escape from the hopeless struggle with bishops and king in order to establish a "due form of government both civil and ecclesiastical." The other was that he (and no doubt other men in his position) found "his means heer soe shortened as he shall not be able to continue in that place and employment where he now is." Winthrop was a man of substantial estate, and if his means were shortened, how much more so were those of ordinary men! "This lande," he says, "grows weary of her inhabitants, soe as man is heer of less price amongst us than a horse or sheep. . . . We stand here striving for places of habitation . . . and in ye mean tyme suffer a whole continent as fruitful and convenient for the use of man to lie waste without any improvement." To be free of oppression or to better their fortunes — for these reasons chiefly the first settlers came to America, and from that time to this the poor and oppressed classes of Europe have continued to come for the same reasons.

The first settlers found plenty of freedom in the new world — so much indeed that in the first years it nearly wiped them out. But they were for the most part a hardy lot. As William Bradford said: "They are too delicate and unfitte to beginne new Plantations and Collonies that cannot endure the biting of a muskeeto." They stuck it out, the hardy ones, enduring all things — the mosquitoes and the Indians, the climate, even in some winters near starvation.

Freedom and Responsibility

They stuck it out and established the form of government that seemed to them due and proper. No doubt they were still subjects of the king and limited by the terms of royal charters, but king and Parliament and bishops were three thousand miles away, and efforts on their part to interfere with the due form of government could be ignored or, with sufficient ingenuity, made of slight effect. And if there were in any colony men too cantankerous to submit to the due form of government, they could always get out. In the New World men did not need to stand striving for places of habitation. And so Anne Hutchinson, who, "speaking from a mere motion of the spirit," criticized the ministers for preaching a covenant of works, and Roger Williams, who believed in soul liberty and even went so far as to say that the land belonged to the Indians, got out of Massachusetts Bay, or were forced out, and went to Rhode Island, where another due form of government was easily improvised and set up. And then there was Thomas Hooker, who had no great objection to the due form of government in Massachusetts Bay, but who found his town second to Boston and himself overtopped in influence by Winthrop and Cotton. He and the people of Newtown, therefore, as we are told, began to "have a hankering" after the Connecticut Valley; and in 1634 they requested from the General Court permission to leave Massachusetts Bay, advancing three reasons — "their want of accommodation for their cattle, the fruitfulness and commodiousness of Connecticut, and the *strong bent of their spirits to remove thither.*"

The migration of the people of Newtown to the Connecticut Valley was in miniature a repetition of the migration of the first settlers from England to the New World and the prototype of all the later migrations from the older settlements to the uninhabited hinterland. Whenever people in the older settlements found the conditions of life unsatisfactory, whether for lack of accommodation for their cattle or some other reason, they were apt to have a "hankering" for some more fruitful and commodious region farther west. Nothing then restrained them from following the "strong bent of their spirits"; and so for three centuries the frontier of settlement was always moving on — into the up-country of Virginia, into western New York and Pennsylvania, over the Alleghenies into the vast and fertile woodland and prairie country of the Middle West, across the Rockies to the Pacific coast. The difficulties and hardships encountered in this quest for new fortunes were many, and the conditions of life on the edge of the frontier were often hazardous and always bleak and primitive. But every successive frontier was a new "new world" which offered to its first settlers essentially the same advantages that New England and Virginia offered to the first settlers from England. It offered them freedom — free land, so that they need not stand striving for places of habitation; freedom from the social and religious conventions and restraints of a more settled society; and freedom within broad limits to establish a due form of government, a government that seemed to them suitable and adequate for people living on terms of equality and in something close to a primitive state of nature.

The decisive factors in securing so much freedom and equality for the people of the United States were the country's geographic isolation from Europe, its vast extent, and its rich and seemingly unlimited natural resources. It is related that an Englishman riding from New York to San Francisco, having after a two days' journey finally arrived at Santa Fe, remarked that the discovery of America by Columbus seemed in no way remarkable, since it was difficult to see how anyone could have missed it. The people of the United States have never been troubled by the problem of *Lebensraum*. There has always been room enough; until recently there has always been (and this is the essential

Freedom and Responsibility

point) plenty of free or relatively free land to be had for the taking. Speculators have done their best at various times to buy it up and hold it for monopoly prices, but with slight success. There was always too much of it, and the consequence is that for the greater part of its history the United States has been predominantly a nation of small farmers owning their land in fee simple — farmers to whom the term "tenant" or "peasant" was unknown and to whom it was in no sense applicable.

Benjamin Franklin, with his sure grasp of economic influences, foresaw this development. He noted the fact that industrialized cities of the European type, with their hopelessly impoverished working classes crowded together in slums, could never develop in America so long as any man with a little gumption could go elsewhere and become the independent owner of a farm. It was this situation that defeated every attempt to transplant and perpetuate in the New World the aristocratic social structure and upper-class political domination that prevailed in the old. In Franklin's time there were, it is true, pale replicas of the English class system in most of the colonies. Political control and social prestige were the prerogatives of a few interrelated landowning and merchant families — people of comparative wealth, living in fine houses, who preserved the social amenities and were conversant with the ideas then current among the educated upper classes in England. They thought of themselves as "the better sort" and looked with benevolent condescension on the "populace" of small farmers in the country and artisans and mechanics in the towns. "A poor man," according to a Philadelphia humorist writing in 1775, "has rarely the honor of speaking to a gentleman on any terms and never with familiarity but for a few weeks before election. How many . . . mechanics have been made happy within this fortnight by a shake of the hand, a pleasing smile, and little familiar chat with gentlemen who have not for these seven years past condescended to look at them." [1] But, for all that, poverty and servility in the European sense were virtually unknown, and any young man of character and ability could, as the saying was, "get ahead" and "make something of himself" — could acquire an education (perhaps, signing himself Cassius, write a piece for the newspaper describing a certain condescension in gentlemen), could acquire a little property, and so edge himself, or at all events his children, into the reserved precincts of the "better sort." Even this mild species of unstable distinctions was seriously impaired by the American Revolution, which was as much an uprising of the populace against the better sort as it was an uprising of the better sort against British control, and it virtually disappeared as a political force in 1828 with the election of Andrew Jackson.

The election of Jackson represented the triumph of the masses over the classes, of the agricultural democracy of the newer West and South over the industrial and moneyed aristocracy of the older East, of the untutored backwoodsman over the cultivated and fastidious gentleman and scholar. At the inaugural reception given by the new president, so we are told, "the White House was invaded by a mob of men, women, and boys who stood on chairs in their muddy boots, fought for the refreshments, and trod glass and porcelain underfoot. 'It would have done Mr. Wilberforce's heart good,' wrote an onlooker, 'to have seen a stout black wench eating in this free country a jelly with a gold spoon in the President's house.' Jackson was glad to escape by a window; and the mob was drawn off like flies to honey, by tubs of punch being placed on the lawn. Washington society thought of the Tuileries on the 10th of August, and shuddered." [2] This episode may be taken to symbolize the

[1] Charles and Mary Beard, *The Rise of American Civilization*, I, 131.
[2] S. E. Morison and H. S. Commager, *The Growth of the American Republic*, 355. [Edition of 1930.]

Freedom and Responsibility

fact that the Middle West was emerging as the central and dominant political force in the United States, and that the rough-and-ready and unabashed freedom and equality of the frontier would make short shrift of ceremony, of distinctions of rank and office, and of the inherited European code of gentility and good manners so highly prized and carefully observed by the better sort.

Such were the essential aspects of the historical experience of the American people that have had a fundamental influence in shaping their ideas about freedom and equality, the function of the government, and the liberty and responsibility of the individual. Since there was for so long a time more fertile land than there were people to cultivate it, it was always relatively easy for the common man to make his own way and pay his own score, unassisted by *noblesse oblige* or communal charity and without benefit of a watchful, paternalistic government: always relatively easy, therefore, for the common man to be and to feel independent, a free man and be damned to you, stranger! Since the people were always on the move from the more settled to the undeveloped regions of the country, successive generations of common men were forced to discard settled customs and fixed habits, to break with family ties and old associations, and, relying on their own initiative and common sense, to reshape social institutions and forms of governments to suit the practical needs of life in new and relatively primitive conditions. In few countries have the common people been so little hampered by tradition in their thought and action, or had so often to adapt their lives to new and often hazardous conditions, or had so often the opportunity to follow the bent of their spirits in framing fundamental constitutional laws and new forms of governments. It is this peculiar historical experience that has disposed the American people to emphasize the freedom and responsibility of the individual and to minimize the function and authority of the government: that is to say, to take it for granted that freedom of thought and conduct is the natural right of the individual, and that government, so far from being something transcendent or divine, is essentially a homespun affair, a convenient committee appointed by the people to perform certain specified communal services, and in the nature of the case bound not to go beyond its instructions.

This conception of the function of government and the freedom and responsibility of the individual, although firmly enough grounded in the historical experience of the American people, is also supported by a political philosophy — a philosophy clearly formulated at the very time when the United States became an independent nation, and purporting to set forth the imprescriptible rights of all men and the essential purpose of all just governments. The confidence of the people of the United States in the rightness of their institutions and freedoms, sufficiently great in any case, is therefore all the greater because they can be reminded every Fourth of July that their institutions and freedoms are the kind of institutions and freedoms best suited to all mankind because prescribed by the law of nature and the will of God.

The natural rights political philosophy was of European origin. The Protestant Reformation was based on the doctrine of justification by faith — the doctrine that the individual becomes a good man by adhering to the law of God rather than by submitting to the laws and conventions of society. In the seventeenth century this doctrine was employed to justify the English revolution against the established authority of church and king, and at that time the law of God was often identified with the law of nature. But it was in the eighteenth century, in connection with the revolt against the despotic power of kings claiming to rule by divine right and supported by a privileged aristocracy of priests and nobles, that the natural rights philosophy was the most clearly formulated, and was given official sanction, as one may say, by the French Declaration of the Rights of Man and the Citizen and the American Declaration of Independence.

In the Declaration of Independence Jefferson expressed what he called "the common sense of the subject" in the following brief passage:

> We hold these truths to be self-evident; that all men are created equal; that they are endowed by their Creator with inherent and unalienable rights; that among these are life, liberty, and the pursuit of happiness; that to secure these rights governments are instituted among men, deriving their just powers from the consent of the governed; that whenever any form of government becomes destructive of these ends, it is the right of the people to alter or to abolish it, and to institute a new government, laying its foundation on such principles and organizing its powers in such form as to them shall seem most likely to effect their safety and happiness.

This statement may be reduced to four fundamental principles: (1) that the universe, including man, is subject to the law of nature, which is a revelation of the will of God; (2) that all men have certain natural or God-given rights; (3) that governments exist to secure these rights; and (4) that all just governments derive their authority from the consent of the governed.

This is the essence of the political philosophy formulated in the eighteenth century to justify the liberal-democratic revolution of modern times. It was revolutionary only in the sense that it was a reinterpretation in secular and liberal terms of the Christian doctrine of the origin, nature, and destiny of man. It denied that man is naturally prone to evil and error, and for that reason incapable, apart from the compulsion of state and church, of arriving at the truth or living the good life. It affirmed, on the contrary, that men are endowed by their creator with reason in order that they may progressively discover that which is true, and with conscience in order that they may be disposed, in the measure of their enlightenment, to follow that which is good. If Jefferson and his contemporaries entertained a somewhat too optimistic faith in the natural intelligence and goodness of men, the reason is that they were living at a time when in most countries men were too much governed — a time when the oppressions suffered by the majority of men were those imposed by the organized authority of church and state. For the majority of men, liberty could therefore be most easily conceived in terms of the emancipation of the individual from governmental constraint, and in order to justify such emancipation it was necessary to assume that men were by nature sufficiently rational and sufficiently good for the restraints of law and custom safely to be reduced to a minimum.

For Jefferson and his contemporaries the essential freedoms were, naturally enough, those which had been the most commonly denied. Of these, there were three principal ones — freedom of opinion in order that the truth might prevail; freedom of occupation and economic enterprise in order that careers might be open to talent; and freedom from arbitrary government in order that no man might be compelled against his will. These freedoms were precisely what Jefferson meant by "liberty" as one of the inherent and inalienable rights of man, and it was through the fullest enjoyment of these freedoms that the "pursuit of happiness" would be the most likely to result in the greatest happiness for the greatest number of men. And so we arrive at the central idea of the natural rights philosophy in respect to the function of government and the freedom and responsibility of the individual: the happy idea that the best way to secure the inalienable rights of man is just to leave the individual as free as possible to do what he likes, and that accordingly no form of government can secure them so well as the one that governs least.

The natural rights philosophy made its way in America with far less opposition than it did in Europe. It was accepted as a convenient theory for justifying the political separation of the American colonies from Great Britain; but with that object attained no further revolution of serious import, such as occurred in France, was required to bring the social and political institutions of the United States into harmony with the philosophy that presided at its birth as an independent nation. The state and Federal constitutions were scarcely more than a codification of colonial institutions with the Parliament and king left out, and the natural rights philosophy of the Declaration of Independence was accepted without much opposition as the obvious and necessary foundation of the new political structure. If the colonies had ever been governed by a king, it was only by a king *in absentia* exercising a merely nominal control. Monarchical absolutism and the theory of divine right, the vested interest of a ruling landed aristocracy based on birth, the moral and political influence of an organized state religion — none of these obstacles to political and social democracy, which had to be overcome in all European countries, was ever in any real sense a part of the American political practice or tradition. The people of the United States never had to live with the resistant survivals of an *ancien régime:* never had, like the British, to place a king in cold storage in order to keep a Pretender off their backs, or, like the French, to make terms with powerful royalist and clerical parties openly or secretly bent on destroying the republic. The natural rights philosophy was therefore accepted by the people of the United States, as one may say, without debate and by a rising vote. It seemed to them, as Jefferson said, merely the "common sense of the subject"; and it seemed to them the common sense of the subject because it was scarcely more than an ideological description of institutions and a way of life to which they had long been accustomed and to which they were entirely devoted.

3

In a famous passage of *The Decline and Fall of the Roman Empire* Edward Gibbon said that the second century A.D. was "the period in the history of the world, during which the condition of the human race was most happy and prosperous." It may now be said that during the eighteenth and nineteenth centuries the people of the United States enjoyed a greater degree of political liberty, social equality, and widely based material prosperity than has ever fallen to the lot of any other people. This happy state was won, not by desperate struggles against the oppressions of men, but by unremitting effort to appropriate the rich resources of a great and undeveloped country. That task could be accomplished with a minimum of governmental control and a maximum of individual freedom of thought and enterprise. It may be said, therefore, that our political freedom and social equality were the casual and lavish gift of nature rather than anything won by war or revolution or devised to conform with a reasoned theory of politics and society. We are not on that account any the less attached to our form of government and to the freedoms associated with it. On the contrary, we are profoundly attached to them. We are attached to them for many reasons, no doubt — because they have emerged so naturally from the everyday experience of living and making a living, because they have for so long a time worked so well, because they are sustained by instinctive emotional responses and unconscious habitual ways of behaving, and because nothing in our history or tradition provides us with a model of any other political or social system. But we are also attached to them because of

Freedom and Responsibility

a profound conviction, of which we are perhaps not often aware, that the republican form of government is, as Jefferson said, the only one that is not eternally at open or secret war with the natural rights of mankind, or at all events with those familiar rights and privileges which we regard as in some sense natural because by long habituation they seem to us so imprescriptibly American.

We are much attached to our government and to our freedoms, but we have often taken them a little too much for granted as familiar and replaceable possessions which we may use or abuse as the occasion demands. We have been so rich in freedoms that they have seemed to us expendable; we have so much the sense of liberty unrestrained that it often seems permissible to take liberties with our liberty. Our sense of freedom and of self-direction are ingrained, but so is our impulse to direct action: naturally enough, perhaps, since both derive from the same experience — the experience of a people who for three centuries have been mainly engaged in the practical task of subduing a virgin continent to human use and habitation with a minimum of governmental authority either to assist or to restrain them. To get the immediate practical task done with a minimum of palaver, a minimum of attention to red tape or strict rule of law or rights abstractly defined, is apt to seem to us the obvious because it has so often been the necessary procedure. Whether it has been a matter of clearing the forest or exterminating the redskins, organizing a government or exploiting it for private advantage, building railroads for the public good or rigging the market in order to milk them for private profit, establishing free schools by law or placing illegal restraints on the freedom of teaching, conferring on Negroes their God-given constitutional rights or making sure they do not vote, applauding the value of temperance or perceiving the convenience of bootlegging — whatever the immediate task may be, the short cut, the ready-made device for dealing with it, is apt to seem to us good enough so long as it gets the business done. Throughout our history ruthlessness and humane dealing, respect for law and right and disregard of them, have run side by side: in almost equal degree we have exhibited the temper of conformity and of revolt, the disposition to submit voluntarily to law and custom when they serve our purposes and to ignore them when they cease to do so.

Until comparatively recently all this has served us well enough. We were so rich that we could afford to be careless and extravagant. We could afford to exploit our natural resources with a maximum of waste for immediate ends and with a minimum of care for their long-time uses. We could afford to regard liberty and equality as complementary terms indicating identical values on the opposite sides of the same coin. We could assume that unrestrained individual enterprise would result in the maximum production of wealth and in as equitable a distribution of it as the natural qualities and defects of men permitted. We could afford, in normal times at least, to regard international affairs as a formality to be attended to by the Secretary of State; and in normal times we could afford to take domestic politics casually, even cynically, as a diverting game played according to understood rules of rhetoric and melodrama — played with gusto, indeed, but for low stakes that, however it came out and whoever won, would not seriously injure business or interfere with any man's chance for getting his own back. We could afford, in short, to let the public business ride, trusting that if every man got what he could and spent it as he liked, the total assets and liabilities, with a generous margin left for profit and loss, would balance well enough in the final accounting.

Although all of this has served us well enough in the past, unfortunately that happy time of universal prosperity, of careers open to talent, of the maximum of freedom of en-

Freedom and Responsibility

terprise conjoined with a minimum of responsibility, is now passed beyond recovery.

In the final revision of *The American Commonwealth* James Bryce, a good friend and great admirer of Americans and their institutions, ventured to make a prophecy:

> There is a part of the Atlantic where the westward-speeding steam-vessel always expects to encounter fogs. On the fourth or fifth day of the voyage while still in bright sunlight, one sees at a distance a long, low, dark gray line across the bows, and is told that this is the first of the fog banks that have to be traversed. Presently the vessel is upon the cloud, and rushes into its chilling embrace, not knowing what perils of icebergs may be shrouded within its encompassing gloom.
>
> So America, in her swift onward progress, sees, looming on the horizon and now no longer distant, a time of mists and shadows, wherein dangers may be concealed whose form and magnitude she can scarcely yet conjecture. As she fills up her Western regions with inhabitants, she sees the time approach when all of the best land . . . will have been occupied, and when the land now under cultivation will have been so far exhausted as to yield scantier crops even to more expensive culture. Although transportation may also have become cheaper, the price of food will rise; farms will be less easily obtained and will need more capital to work them with profit; the struggle for existence will become more severe. And while the outlet which the West now provides for the overflow of the great cities will have become less available, the cities will have grown immensely more populous; pauperism . . . may be more widely spread; and even if wages do not sink work may be less abundant. In fact, the chronic evils and problems of old societies and crowded countries, such as we see them today in Europe, will have reappeared in this new soil, while the demand of the multitude to have a larger share in the nation's collective wealth may well have grown more insistent.
>
> High economic authorities pronounce that the beginnings of this time of pressure lie not more than twenty years ahead. . . . It may be the time of trial for democratic institutions.

The American Political Tradition

This was in 1914. Fifteen years later the United States rushed into the encompassing gloom of the great depression; and it is obvious that the problems that now confront us, apart from the additional problems created by the war, are in essentials those that Bryce foresaw. Land is no longer to be had for the taking. The necessary job is no longer ready and waiting for the young man who needs it. Our potential wealth is still immense, but we can no longer count on unrestrained individual enterprise to make it fully available or to get it properly distributed. So long as mass unemployment is a major social disaster we cannot afford to take domestic politics as a diverting game played for low stakes; nor can we, at a time when men can fly bombing planes from New York to Hong Kong in less time than it took Ben Franklin to travel from Philadelphia to New York, afford to ignore international politics in the hope of living securely in isolation from other nations.

We are living in the time of pressure that Bryce foretold, and the pressure appears to take the form of a profoundly disturbing paradox. We seem to be offered a choice between depression and mass unemployment as the price of peace, and total war as the price of expansion and general prosperity. Are we, then, limited to this choice? Can we cure one serious evil only by embracing another and worse one? This paradox, unless it be resolved, will surely wreck our institutions and destroy our freedoms, and we cannot resolve it by letting things ride. Hitherto our freedoms have been the lavish gift of the country we inhabit; we can preserve them only by our own effort — only by a far more serious and intelligent attention to public affairs than we have hitherto been willing or found it necessary to give to them. If we do that, we shall find, I think, that it is necessary for us to insist somewhat less stubbornly upon our individual freedoms, and to recognize somewhat less grudgingly our communal responsibilities.

Freedom and Responsibility

It may be worth while, then, to examine in some detail our various liberties, in the hope of disclosing what is essential in them and must be preserved, and what is inessential and may safely be renounced. In the next two lectures I shall deal with the most fundamental of our freedoms, the one that is essential to all the others — freedom of the mind.

II

Freedom of Speech and Press

> Congress shall make no law . . . abridging the freedom of speech, or of the press; or the right of the people peacefully to assemble, and to petition the government for a redress of grievances.
>
> *First Amendment to the Constitution*

THE TENTH AMENDMENT to the Constitution states that "the powers not delegated by the Constitution to the United States, nor prohibited by it to the States, are reserved to the States respectively, *or to the people.*" For our purpose the qualifying phrase "to the people" is more important than the rest of the statement, because it discloses the fundamental principle on which all of our governments, state and Federal, are grounded — the principle that in the last analysis all powers are reserved to the people. We might then, without changing our system of government in any way, add another amendment to all of our constitutions: "The powers not delegated to the governments by the people, nor prohibited by them to the individual, are reserved to the individual." This is only another way of saying that our Government purports to be a government of free men, and that restraints on the individual's freedom to act and to speak for himself are self-imposed because defined in laws made by the will of the people.

But the will of the people is an intangible thing. "The people" comprises many people — many individuals with diverse and conflicting desires and wills. How can this conflict of wills be reconciled? The practical way in a republic is by majority vote. If the majority wills to prohibit, for example, the sale and manufacture of spirituous liquors, then the minority has to renounce that right; but how then can we say that the minority is not bound against its will or subject to restraints not self-imposed? Rousseau had a solution for this difficulty. He maintained that all members of society have agreed, by an original social compact, to submit their individual wills in particular measures to the general will. When, therefore, you and I cast our votes for or against a proposed measure, we are not really voting for or against the measure; we are merely voting to determine what the general will is in respect to that measure. If we vote against it, and it turns out that the majority voted for it, we are not defeated, but only enlightened; and since we now know that the majority is for the measure we are for it too, because we have, by the original social compact, already agreed to submit our individual wills to the general will as soon as we know what that will is.

Does all this sound like hocus-pocus — a dialectical runaround? It does, a little. But, after all, does it not describe well enough, although with a good deal of verbal gymnastics, what we actually do and think when we vote for or against this or that measure, or for or against this or that party? When we have an election, more especially a presidential election, the Democrats make a tremendous hullabaloo about the country's going to ruin if the Republicans win, and the Republicans make an equally alarming hullabaloo about the country's going to ruin if "that man" is elected again. But when the shouting is over and the votes are counted, what do we do then? All of us, defeated and despondent minority no less than triumphant and elated majority, take the count, accept the decision, and go about our business. And no one really thinks that the country is going to ruin, or that anyone is going to be deprived of his natural rights because the laws will be made for some time by a party he did not will to place in power. And why do we act and think in this way if it be not that all of us have agreed, not in the explicit terms of an original compact perhaps, but in terms of an implicit understanding consciously or unconsciously subscribed to, that the general will of the nation is to be determined by majority vote, and that all our rights and liberties can best be secured by submitting voluntarily to the will of the majority?

However that may be, and whatever fine-spun theories we may devise to resolve or obscure the difficulty, there is no use blinking the fact that the will of the majority is not the same thing as the will of all. Majority rule works well only so long as the minority is willing to accept the will of the majority as the will of the nation and let it go at that. Generally speaking, the minority will be willing to let it go at that so long as it feels that its essential interests and rights are not fundamentally different from those of the current majority, and so long as it can, in any case, look forward with confidence to mustering enough votes within four or sixteen years to become itself the majority and so redress the balance. But if it comes to pass that a large minority feels that it has no such chance, that it is a fixed and permanent minority and that another group or class with rights and interests fundamentally hostile to its own is in permanent control, then goverment by majority vote ceases in any sense to be government by the will of the people for the good of all, and becomes government by the will of some of the people for their own interests at the expense of the others.

The founders of the republic were fully aware of this danger. Jefferson accepted the device of majority vote because it was the only practicable method of registering the will of the people; but he was not so blind as to think that the majority was always right, or that it would never abuse its power. "I believe," he said, "that there exists a right that is independent of force; . . . that justice is the fundamental law of society; that the majority, oppressing an individual, is guilty of a crime, abuses its strength, and by acting on the principle of the strongest breaks up the foundations of society." Jefferson and his contemporaries had faith in republican government because they believed that it provided the best security for the natural rights of men against the tyranny of kings and aristocrats. But they were fully aware that even in a republic the natural rights of men need to be safeguarded against another sort of tyranny — the tyranny of the majority. Against the tyranny of the majority, or at all events against hasty and ill-considered action by the majority, the founding fathers endeavored, therefore, to erect adequate safeguards.

One of these safeguards is to be found in the organization of government and the distribution of powers within it — an organization based on the grand negative principle of checks and balances. But there were certain rights of the individual that the founding fathers regarded as sacred and imprescriptible — rights that no government, even one founded on the will of the people, could ever justly deny. This idea, that natural right is superior to prescriptive law, is indeed fundamental in the political philosophy formulated in the eighteenth century to justify the liberal-democratic revolution of modern times. It was clearly set forth in the French Declaration of the Rights of Man and the Citizen. Jefferson expressed it in the Declaration of Independence by saying that governments are instituted among men to secure the natural and inalienable rights of man, and that when any government becomes destructive of these rights it is the right of the people to alter or to abolish it. This central idea, with much of the phraseology in which Jefferson expressed it, appears in all our constitutions. To this day, therefore, the natural rights philosophy is implicit

Freedom of Speech and Press

in our system of government. It still stands, as one may say, in the entrance ways of all our constitutions, safeguarding the imprescriptible rights of man.

The most important of these rights, the one that is essential to all the rest and the foundation of democratic government as we understand it, is freedom of the mind — the right of every person, as the Connecticut Constitution puts it, to "speak, write, and publish his sentiments on all subjects, being responsible for the abuse of that liberty."

A good many years ago, when Mussolini was much admired for clearing the streets of beggars and making the trains run on time, a good lady said to me that she couldn't understand all this palaver about freedom of speech and of the press. Isn't everyone, she asked, always free to say what he thinks? Of course, she added, one must be prepared to take the consequences. I was unable on the spur of the moment to find an answer to that one. But it has since occurred to me that the good lady was more profoundly right than she realized. Democratic government rests on the assumption that the people are capable of governing themselves better than any one or any few can do it for them; but this in turn rests on the further assumption that if the people are free to think, speak, and publish their sentiments on any subject, the consequences will be good. Well, sometimes they are and sometimes not. If we have faith in democracy, we get over this inconvenient fact by saying that by and large and in the long run the consequences will be good. But the point is that if we accept democracy we must accord to everyone the right to think, speak, and publish his sentiments on any subject; and in that case we must indeed be prepared to take the consequences, whatever they may turn out to be.

It will be well, therefore, to examine this fundamental right with some care, in order to see, first, why Jefferson and his contemporaries were so profoundly convinced that the consequences would always and everywhere be good; and, secondly, whether we are still justified, in the light of a longer practical experience, in supposing that by and large and in the long run the consequences will at least be good enough to go on with.

2

The preoccupation of eighteenth-century philosophers with intellectual freedom was nowhere so great perhaps as in France, and it was in France that the natural rights philosophy which provided a theoretical justification for it was the most elaborately and clearly formulated. The reasons for this are easily understood. It is not so much because Frenchmen, as has sometimes been maintained, are more liberty-loving or more logically minded than other people, but rather because there was in France a great number of extraordinarily gifted writers of all sorts who had themselves suffered oppression from church and state for their opinions, and who were, partly for that reason, passionately concerned with the manifest inequities of the existing social system.

The best-known and the most valiant defender of the freedom of the mind was Voltaire. It is difficult to think of the mind of Voltaire, whose published works run to ninety volumes, as ever having been much restrained, and it is alarming to think how many volumes his works might have run to if it had been entirely unhampered. But all the same it is a fact that in order to avoid the penalties imposed by church and state for seditious writing, Voltaire took the trouble to publish many of his works in Holland or England, thought it safer to publish some of them under a false name, and found it more convenient to live much of his life close to the French frontier, where he could at a moment's notice slip across the border into Switzerland.

If, then, Voltaire became a passionate defender of the

freedom of the mind, it was partly because he himself had been much harassed for the lack of it. Partly; but not entirely, or chiefly. He had always present in his mind the fates of Giordano Bruno, of Galileo, and of many obscure persons, such as Calas in his own time, who had suffered unspeakable torture and death for their religious faith. He had always in mind the illuminating fact that in England everyone, as he said, was permitted to go to Heaven in his own way, and no one the worse for it, and that the incomparable Isaac Newton, who had discovered the invariable laws of nature, instead of suffering the fate of Galileo was proclaimed and honored by church and state as a benefactor of mankind. He had always and especially in mind the essential teaching of history as he conceived it — that the progress of knowledge and the arts and the happiness of mankind had been the greatest in those periods, those "four happy ages," when men were the most free to speak the truth, whereas ignorance and superstition and oppression were universal in Europe during the long Dark Age of ecclesiastical domination.

This may have been, and in many respects was, a false reading of history. But for Voltaire, and for most of his contemporaries, it was the correct reading; and if he and his contemporaries regarded freedom of the mind as the essential freedom, on which all other freedoms rested, it was because they were convinced by the history of mankind that the denial of this freedom had always retarded, and would always retard, the advancement of civilization. They accepted the biblical injunction that the truth shall make you free. They agreed with Abélard that "by doubting we are led to questioning, and by questioning we arrive at the truth." They were profoundly convinced, therefore, that if men were free to inquire about all things, to doubt and discuss all things, to form opinions on the basis of knowledge and evidence, and to utter their opinions freely, the competition of knowledge and opinion in the market of rational discourse would ultimately banish ignorance and superstition and enable men to shape their conduct and their institutions in conformity with the fundamental and invariable laws of nature and the will of God.

The freedom of the individual mind from the compulsion of church and state was thus a right that Voltaire and Jefferson and their contemporaries derived in the first instance from political experience and the teaching of history. But for them it had a higher validity than that. It was a fundamental article of faith in their religious or philosophical conception of God and nature and of the relation of man to both. For most eighteenth-century philosophers the laws of nature and the will of God were the same thing, or rather the laws of nature were an intended and adequate expression of the will of God. Natural law, said the French philosopher Volney, is "the constant and regular order of facts by which God rules the universe; the order which his wisdom presents to the sense and reason of men, to serve them as an equal and common rule of conduct, and to guide them, without distinction of race or sect, towards perfection and happiness." In the eighteenth century God the Father had become attenuated into God the First Cause or Creator. Having at the beginning of things constructed the universe on a rational plan as a convenient habitation for mankind, the Creator had withdrawn from the immediate and arbitrary control of human affairs, leaving men to work out their own salvation as best they could. But this they could do very well, because the beneficent intentions of God were revealed, not in sacred scriptures, but in the great open book of nature, which all men endowed with the light of reason could read and interpret. The mysterious ways in which God moved to perform his wonders, so far from being known through official and dogmatic pronouncements of church and state, were to be progressively discovered by the free play of human reason upon accumulated and verifiable knowledge. The free play of human reason, given time enough, could therefore discover the invariable laws of nature and nature's God and, by bringing the ideas and the institutions of men into conformity with them, find the way, as Volney said, to perfection and happiness.

This conception of God and nature and of the relation of man to both provided the eighteenth-century philosophers with their faith in the worth and dignity of the individual man and the efficacy of human reason. The eighteenth century was the moment in history when men experienced the first flush and freshness of the idea that man is master of his own fate; the moment in history, also, when this emancipating idea, not yet brought to the harsh test of experience, could be accepted with unclouded optimism. Never had the universe seemed less mysterious, more simply constructed, more open and visible and eager to yield its secrets to common-sense questions. Never had the nature of man seemed less perverse, or the intelligence and will of men more pliable to rational persuasion. Never had social and political evils seemed so wholly the result of ignorance and superstition, or so easily corrected by the spread of knowledge and the construction of social institutions on a rational plan. The first task of political science was to discover the natural rights of man, the second to devise the form of government best suited to secure them. And for accomplishing this high task, for creating and maintaining a society founded on justice and equality, the essential freedom was freedom of the mind.

The extraordinary faith of the early prophets of democracy in the efficacy of the human reason and in the native disposition of men to be guided by it is well brought out by John Stuart Mill in reference to his father, a hard-headed man if there ever was one. "So complete," says Mill, "was my father's reliance on the influence of reason over the minds of mankind, whenever it was allowed to reach them, that he felt that all would be gained if the whole population were taught to read, if all sorts of opinions were allowed to be addressed to them by word and writing, and if by means of the suffrage they could nominate a legislature to give effect to the opinions they adopted." It was as simple as that.

In practice we find it somewhat less simple, no doubt; but to this day our faith in democracy, if we have any, has the same ideological basis as that of James Mill. Since primitive times virtually all religious or social systems have attempted to maintain themselves by forbidding free criticism and analysis either of existing institutions or of the doctrine that sustains them; of democracy alone is it the cardinal principle that free criticism and analysis by all and sundry is the highest virtue. In its inception modern democracy was, therefore, a stupendous gamble for the highest stakes. It offered long odds on the capacity and integrity of the human mind. It wagered all it had that the freest exercise of the human reason would never disprove the proposition that only by the freest exercise of the human reason can a tolerably just and rational society ever be created.

The play is still on, and we are still betting on freedom of the mind, but the outcome seems now somewhat more dubious than it did in Jefferson's time, because a century and a half of experience makes it clear that men do not in fact always use their freedom of speech and of the press in quite the rational and disinterested way they are supposed to. An examination of freedom of the mind in practice should enable us, therefore, to estimate the odds for and against the theory somewhat more accurately than Jefferson and his contemporaries were able to do.

3

The democratic doctrine of freedom of speech and of the press, whether we regard it as a natural and inalienable right or not, rests upon certain assumptions. One of these is that men desire to know the truth and will be disposed to be guided by it. Another is that the sole method of arriving at the truth in the long run is by the free competition of opinion in the open market. Another is that, since men will inevitably differ in their opinions, each man must be permitted to urge, freely and even strenuously, his own opinion, provided he accords to others the same right. And the final assumption is that from this mutual toleration and comparison of diverse opinions the one that seems the most rational will emerge and be generally accepted.

The classic expression of this procedure and this attitude of mind is the saying attributed, incorrectly it may be, to Voltaire: "I disagree absolutely with what you say, but I will defend to the death your right to say it." For me these famous words always call up, at first, an agreeable picture — the picture of two elderly gentlemen, in powdered wigs and buckled shoes, engaged over their toddy in an amiable if perhaps somewhat heated discussion about the existence of the deity. But when I try to fit the phrase into the free competition of opinion as it actually works out in our present democratic society, the picture fades out into certain other pictures, some even more agreeable, others much less so. The more agreeable picture might be that of Pierre and Marie Curie working day and night for four years in their leaky laboratory for the sole purpose of discovering the truth about pitchblende. The less agreeable picture might be that of some business tycoon placing self above service by purveying misinformation about the value of certain stocks which he wishes to palm off on the public. Or it might be the picture of a newspaper editor blue-penciling a story altogether true and needing to be known, because it does not have a sufficiently sensational "news value." Or it might be the picture of some fruity-throated radio announcer availing himself every day of his inalienable right of misrepresenting the merits of a certain toothpaste. Or else the picture of a Congressional committee exercising its freedom of the press to denounce as Communists certain worthy men and women who are not Communists by any reasonable definition of Communism, because they have exercised their freedom of speech to say a good word for the labor unions or the Spanish Loyalists, or because they have subscribed for and read the *Nation,* the *New Republic,* or the *Daily Worker.*

These instances may serve to make vivid the fact that freedom of speech does not travel exclusively on a one-way street marked "Search for Truth." It often enough travels on a one-way street marked "Private Profit," or on another marked "Anything to Win the Election." Most often, no doubt, it travels every which way on the broad unmarked highway of diverse human activities. This is only to say that the right of free speech cannot be considered to any good purpose apart from the concrete situations in which it is exercised; and in all such situations the relevant questions are, who is exercising the right, by what means, and for what purposes? I have already quoted the Connecticut Constitution of 1818: "Every citizen may speak, write, and publish his sentiments on all subjects, being responsible for the abuse of that liberty." All of our constitutions recognize that there may be abuses of the liberty that need to be defined and prohibited by law. The relevant question always is, what abuses are sufficiently grave to be prohibited by law? And the most relevant and difficult question of all is, in limiting the right because it is abused, at what point precisely does the limitation of the right become a greater evil than the abuse because it threatens to destroy the right altogether?

The classic instance of this dilemma arises in connection with the Communists and the Fascists — a dilemma that may be stated in the following way:

Democratic government rests on the right of the people to govern themselves, and therefore on the right of all citizens to advocate freely in speech and writing a modification of the existing form of government — the right of advocating, let us say, the abolition of the House of Representatives, or the election of a president for life. Well, the Communists and the Fascists avail themselves of the right of free speech to advocate the abolition of the democratic form of government altogether, and they maintain that since it cannot be done by persuasion and voting it should be done by force. Is this an abuse of the right of free speech? Is the democratic right of free speech to be accorded to those whose avowed aim is to destroy democratic government and free speech as a part of it? Are we expected to be loyal to the principle of free speech to the point where, writhing in pain among its worshipers, it commits suicide? That is certainly asking a lot.

It is asking too much so long as we remain in the realm of logical discourse. The program of the Fascists, and of the Communists in so far at least as the preliminaries of political reform are concerned, is based on an appeal to force rather than to persuasion. Their own principles teach us that it is logical for them to resist suppression, but merely impudent for them to resent it. Very well, then, since that is their program, let us stop talking, appeal to force, and see which is the stronger. Freedom of speech is for those who are *for* it — for those who are willing to accept it and abide by it as a political method; and I can see no reason why a democratic government should not defend its existence by force against internal as well as against external enemies whose avowed aim is to destroy it.

But strict logic is a poor counselor of political policy, and I can see no practical virtue in a syllogistic solution of the problem of Communist or Fascist propaganda. Freedom of speech can neither be suppressed by argument nor supported by suppressing argument. The real danger is not that Communists and Fascists will destroy our democratic government by free speaking, but that our democratic government, through its own failure to cure social evils, will destroy itself by breeding Communists and Fascists. If we can by the democratic method sufficiently alleviate social injustice, freedom of speech will sufficiently justify itself; if not, freedom of speech will in any case be lost in the shuffle.

It is in connection with social injustices that the question of free speech raises practical rather than theoretical problems. These problems concern the abuses of free speech committed by those who employ freedom of speech, not to destroy democratic government, but to serve their own interests by distorting the truth or betraying the public interest. That such abuses exist no one denies, and that some of them should be prohibited by law no one has ever denied. No one believes in the freedom of speech that issues in libel and slander. The practical question is, are our laws against slander and libel well adapted to meet the modern ingenious methods of insidious within-the-law vilification?

Or, to take a different case, no one can deny that much of our modern advertising is essentially dishonest; and it can hardly be maintained that to lie freely and all the time for private profit is not to abuse the right of free speech, whether it be a violation of the law or not. But again the practical question is, how much lying for private profit is to be permitted by law? Vendors of toothpaste say every day that their particular brands will cure bad breath, re-

Freedom of Speech and Press

store to the teeth the original brilliance of the enamel, and thereby enable anyone to recover the lost affection of husband or wife or boy or girl friend. What to do about it? Well, better let it go. The law cannot do everything; it must assume that people have some intelligence; and if the toothpaste is harmless, and the people are so ignorant as not to know the obvious facts of life (one of which is that high-powered advertising is a kind of mental test of the gullibility factor of the people) , well, it is too bad maybe, but it is not a responsibility that the law can wisely assume. Liberty is the right of anyone to do whatever does not injure others; and it does not injure anyone to use the permitted brands of toothpaste, even if salt water or powdered chalk would do him just as much good besides being much less expensive.

It is quite another matter, however, if the systematic lying for private profit or personal advantage does injure others. If the toothpaste destroys the enamel instead of leaving it as it was; if the cosmetic, instead of being harmless, poisons the skin; if published misinformation induces ignorant or gullible people to invest their money in worthless stocks — in such and many similar cases the freedom of the liar to "speak, write, and publish his sentiments" needs to be restrained by law. The number of such laws has increased, is increasing, and will undoubtedly continue to increase. There can be no natural and inalienable right to lie systematically for private profit or personal advantage; and if the individual will not assume the responsibility for being reasonably honest, the government must assume the responsibility of restraining his freedom of speaking and acting for dishonest purposes and to the injury of others. But this raises a question of fundamental importance for the maintenance of democracy and of the freedom of speech and action that are inseparable from it. The question is, how far will it be necessary to go in making laws for curbing the

Freedom and Responsibility

dishonest and protecting the ignorant and gullible? How much ignorance, gullibility, and dishonesty can there be without making it impossible, by any number of laws designed to protect the ignorant and curb the dishonest, to preserve anything that can rightly be called democracy?

Democratic government is self-government, and self-government, if it be more than an empty form, is something far more than the popular election of representatives to make laws regulating everything and thereby to relieve the people of the responsibility for what they do. Whatever the form of government may be, it is not self-government unless the people are mostly intelligent enough and honest enough to do of their own accord what is right and necessary with a minimum of legal compulsion and restraint. Self-government works best, of course, in a small community in which everyone knows everyone else and in which the relations of men are therefore mostly direct and personal. It works well enough in a new and sparsely settled community in which there is room enough for everyone, in which the people do not get in each other's way too much whatever they do, and in which there is a fair chance for every man to get on in life as well as his ability and industry permit.

But we no longer live in such a community. We live in a highly complex and economically integrated community in which the relations of men are largely indirect and impersonal, and the life and fortunes of every citizen are profoundly affected, in ways that are not apparent and cannot be foreseen or avoided, by what others unknown to him are doing or planning to do. In such a community it is increasingly difficult for the honest to be intelligent and informed about what is going on and who is getting away with it, and therefore increasingly easy for the intelligent and informed to push their interests dishonestly under cover of the general ignorance. In such a community, it is obvious, there must be more laws for curbing the dishonest and for pro-

Freedom of Speech and Press

tecting the ignorant and the gullible. But it is equally obvious that self-government cannot be maintained by laws alone, and that if there are too many ignorant and gullible and dishonest people in the community the process of curbing the dishonest and protecting the ignorant may easily reduce the sphere of individual responsibility, and therefore of individual freedom, to the point where self-government in any real sense of the word ceases to exist.

The dishonest, undercover promotion of selfish interests on the part of the intelligent and the informed few thrives on the ignorance and gullibility of the many, and both are intimately related to the means by which information and misinformation can be communicated. In the eighteenth century it was taken for granted by the prophets of liberal democracy that if all men were free to "speak, write, and publish" their sentiments, the means of doing so would be freely available. Any group of citizens could meet in public assembly and argue to their hearts' content. Any man could establish a newspaper and every week air his opinions on all questions. Any man could, in the spirit of Brutus or Publicola, write a piece and get it published in the newspaper, or at slight cost in a penny pamphlet. Any man, if sufficiently high-brow, could write and publish a book. And all intelligent citizens could without too much effort attend the public forums, read the newspapers and many of the most talked-of books and pamphlets, and thereby, such was the theory, keep well abreast of what was being thought and said about public affairs in his community, and so play his proper part in molding public opinion and legislation.

It was not, of course, even in the eighteenth century, quite so simple as that; but today it is far less simple than it was in the eighteenth century. The average citizen still enjoys the inestimable right of freedom of speech and of the press. Any man can express his sentiments without first

Freedom and Responsibility

looking furtively over his shoulder to see if a government spy is in the offing; any man can, so far as the law is concerned, print a newspaper or a book without first submitting it to an official censor. This is the fundamentally important privilege; and no cataloguing of incidental violations of the right can obscure the fact that through the press and the radio detailed information about events, and the most diverse opinions, are with little let or hindrance daily and hourly presented to the people.

Daily and hourly presented to the people — it is this submerging flood of information and misinformation that makes the situation today so much less simple than it was in the eighteenth century. The means of gathering and communicating information about all that is being said and done and thought all over the world have become so perfected that no man can possibly take in, much less assimilate, more than a very small part of it. No man, unless he makes a full-time job of it, can hope to keep abreast of what is being said and done in the world at large, or even in his own country. The average citizen, although free to form and express his opinion, therefore plays a minor role in molding public opinion. His role is not to initiate, but passively to receive information and misinformation and diverse opinions presented to him by those who have access to the means of communication.

The propagation of information and opinion, to be effective under modern conditions, must be organized; and its promoters will have an indifferent success unless they resort to mass production and mass distribution of their wares. The chief instruments of propaganda are the press and the broadcasting stations. No one who does not command a great deal of capital can establish a broadcasting station. Much less, but still a good deal, of capital is required to establish a publishing company or a newspaper. About fifty years ago William Allen White, borrowing a few thousand dollars, established the *Emporia Gazette,* and with the aid of one or two assistants was able to make a go of it — a very good go indeed! But William Allen White was not an average citizen. He was a genius and a Kansan; and even so he told me a few years ago that he could not now, starting from scratch, establish another *Emporia Gazette.* Any man can of course write a letter and get it published in a newspaper; but the chief instruments of propaganda are not readily available to the average citizen. They can be effectively used only by the Government, political parties, and party leaders, wealthy men and business corporations, associations organized for the promotion of specific causes, and the writers of books that publishers find it worth while to publish.

In our society free and impartial discussion, from which the truth is supposed to emerge, is permitted and does exist. But the thinking of the average citizen and his opinion about public affairs is in very great measure shaped by a wealth of unrelated information and by the most diverse ideas that the selective process of private economic enterprise presents to him for consideration — information the truth of which he cannot verify; ideas formulated by persons unknown to him, and too often inspired by economic, political, religious, or other interests that are never avowed.

4

As Jefferson and his contemporaries did, we still believe that self-government is the best form of government and that freedom of the mind is the most important of the rights that sustain it. We are less sure than they were that a beneficent intelligence designed the world on a rational plan for man's special convenience. We are aware that the laws of nature, and especially the laws of human nature, are less easily discovered and applied than they supposed. We have found it more difficult to define the essential rights of man and to secure them by simple institutional forms than they anticipated. We have learned that human reason is not the infallible instrument for recording the truth that they supposed it to be, and that men themselves are less amenable to rational persuasion. Above all we have learned that freedom of speech and of the press may be used to convey misinformation and distort the truth for personal advantage as well as to express and communicate it for the public good. But although we no longer have the unlimited and solvent backing of God or nature, we are still betting that freedom of the mind will never disprove the proposition that only through freedom of the mind can a reasonably just society ever be created.

We may win our bet, but we shall win it only on certain hard conditions. The conditions are that the people by and large be sufficiently informed to hold and express intelligent opinions on public affairs, and sufficiently honest and public-spirited to subordinate purely selfish interests to the general welfare. In so far as the intelligent and informed systematically employ freedom of speech and of the press for personal and antisocial ends, in so far as the mass of the people are so ignorant and ill-informed as to be capable of being fooled all of the time, freedom of speech and of the press loses its chief virtue and self-government is undermined. Self-government, and the freedom of speech and of the press that sustains it, can be maintained by law only in a formal sense; if they are to be maintained in fact the people must have sufficient intelligence and honesty to maintain them with a minimum of legal compulsion.

This heavy responsibility is the price of freedom, and it can be paid only by a people that has a high degree of integrity and intelligence. Neither intelligence nor integrity can be imposed by law. But the native intelligence, and

Freedom of Speech and Press

perhaps the integrity of the people, can be reinforced by law, more especially by laws providing for schools and universities. This brings us to the consideration of another freedom and another responsibility, or rather to a special aspect of freedom and responsibility of the mind — that is to say, freedom of learning and teaching.

III
Freedom of Learning and Teaching

> Knowledge and learning generally diffused through a community being essential to the preservation of a free government, . . . it shall be the duty of the general assembly . . . to provide by law for a system of education, ascending in regular gradation from township schools to a State university, wherein tuition shall be gratis, and equally open to all.
>
> *Constitution of Indiana (1816)*

FREEDOM OF learning and teaching is an essential part of what I have called freedom of the mind. It might be said, indeed, that freedom of the mind and freedom of learning and teaching are indistinguishable — that they are one and the same thing; and in theory and logic that is true. But the terms "learning" and "teaching" have by long custom come to be associated with learning and teaching of a particular sort — the learning and teaching that go on under specially prepared conditions at a certain age in the life of the individual as distinct from the learning and teaching that go on during the rest of his life. Freedom of learning and teaching has to do, therefore, with the formal education, in schools and colleges, that society thinks it desirable to provide for young men and women as a preparation for what is called "real life." This sort of learning and teaching is commonly regarded as of fundamental importance in a democratic society, and it is for this reason that I have thought it worth while to deal with it in a separate lecture.

From time immemorial men have commonly regarded

Freedom of Learning and Teaching

learning as inherently dangerous, and have instinctively understood that, so far as schools are concerned, the danger could be met in one of two ways — either by not having any schools, or by preventing the schools from teaching any but familiar and accepted ideas. William Berkeley, Governor of Virginia in the seventeenth century, preferred the first way. "Thank God," he said, "there are no free schools or printing; . . . for learning has brought disobedience and heresy . . . into the world, and printing has divulged them. . . . God keep us from both." But most men, in Virginia and elsewhere, being either less pessimistic or more courageous than Governor Berkeley, have preferred the second way; have believed that the danger inherent in learning could best be met by schools under proper control teaching the right things — the ideas and beliefs, whether true or not, that would tend to confirm rather than to undermine the established social system. In the long history of civilization there have been relatively few systems of government that accepted in theory and applied in practice the dangerous notion that learning and teaching should be perfectly free. Modern liberal democracy is one of the few. In theory at least, however much or little it may apply the theory in practice, it rests upon the right of the individual to freedom of learning and teaching. On what ground can the right be justified?

In our constitutions and elsewhere the right has commonly been justified both for philosophical and for practical reasons. In all of our constitutions it is declared, by implication at least, to be one of the natural, God-given, and therefore imprescriptible rights of man. And from colonial times and almost by common consent it has been taken for granted that, as the Indiana Constitution of 1816 puts it, "knowledge and learning generally diffused through a community [are] essential for the preservation of a free government." The subject of freedom of learning and teaching may well be considered, therefore, from these two points of view — first from the philosophical and then from the practical point of view.

2

Jefferson and his contemporaries were quite sure that God had created the universe on a rational plan for man's special convenience, and that he had endowed men with reason in order that they might, by progressively discovering the invariable laws of nature, know what they were intended to be and to do. Freedom of the mind, freedom of learning and teaching, could therefore be regarded by them as an imprescriptible right because it was God's appointed way by which men could read the divine revelation and shape their conduct and institutions in accordance with God's will.

This simple philosophy has lost much of its validity for us. We are no longer sure that the universe was created by a beneficent intelligence, or by any intelligence at all. We are not sure that the universe is anything more than the product of blind material forces that for a certain time and for reasons that are obscure happen to be active, and that may after a certain time and for reasons equally obscure become quiescent. We are not sure that man is more than a peculiarly active chance deposit on the surface of a world as indifferent to him as to itself, or that the mind of man is more than a "survival product" appearing in the human organism because useful to it in finding its way around in a hostile environment, or that human reason is more than the perception of discordant experience pragmatically adjusted to a particular purpose and for the time being. Since this may be so, we can no longer with any confidence justify freedom of the mind, freedom of learning and teaching, by saying that it is a God-given imprescriptible right. We can justify it, if at all, not by reference to its antecedents,

Freedom of Learning and Teaching

but only by reference to its consequences. Let us then, keeping whatever private faith we may still have in God or nature, turn to the record of history to see if it can provide us with any good reason for believing that freedom of learning and teaching has some fundamental and enduring significance in the life of man.

Man is not the only creature capable of learning, but he is the only one capable of appropriating for his own use the learning of others; and this garnered knowledge — knowledge of the past and of distant places — enables him, compels him indeed, to create an ideally extended environment beyond the narrow confines of what is immediately perceived and experienced. Primitive men in "prehistoric" times knew very well the region in which they lived, and what their fathers and grandfathers could tell them of events occurring before they were born. But beyond this narrow world of the matter-of-fact was the outer void of space and time, of nature and history. What this void contained the primitive man did not know, but he realized that it must contain something that it was desirable for him to know, since it might aid or thwart his purposes. Inevitably, therefore, the primitive man enlarged his narrow world of matter-of-fact experience imaginatively, projecting into the outer void of nature a complicated structure of magic, and into the outer void of the long time past an epic story of the doings of gods and heroes since the beginning of created things.

Many primitive peoples never passed beyond this imaginary account of nature and history. But some five or six thousand years ago certain peoples were forced, against their will as one may say, to learn something more. For reasons which it is unnecessary to examine here, they developed a more complex and unstable social structure in which the sharp differentiation of classes presented conflicts and inequities too obvious to be ignored and too flagrant to be accepted without question. In due course written records disclosed the disconcerting fact that the event as recorded differed from the event as remembered, that customs once regarded as sacred no longer prevailed, and that, while empires once powerful had disappeared, cities formerly insignificant had acquired great renown. Thus made aware that the life of man is precarious, that his knowledge is limited and his destiny insecure, certain exceptional individuals — a Buddha or a Confucius, a Solomon or a Socrates — were impelled to ask and to attempt to answer all the fundamental questions. What is the true nature of man and the meaning of life? What are the gods that man should be mindful of them? What are the real activities behind appearance in the outward world of nature? What is fact and what fancy in the epic story? What is conventional and passing and what is permanent and desirable in social arrangements and individual behavior?

With these questions once posed, learning could no longer be confined to the preservation and transmission of what was accepted as true. For certain exceptional individuals it became an end in itself — an attempt to distinguish the true from the false in the inherited tradition and to add something more to the accumulated store of verifiable or more rationally grounded knowledge. Philosophy and mathematics, history and the social studies, literature and the arts, natural science and technology, as they have developed during the ages, are but corrections and elaborations of primitive magic and the epic story — progressive efforts to find out what exists and is occurring in the outer void of the physical universe, and what has existed and has occurred in the outer void of the long time past. And the general result of this progressive effort, during the last five or six thousand years, has been to substitute for the medicine man's magic the matter-of-fact structure of natural sci-

Freedom of Learning and Teaching

ence, and for the poet's epic story the historian's verified account of man's origin and activities.

All of our superiority is in this accumulated and transmitted store of learning and the consequent power it confers upon us. The native intelligence of the modern man is probably no greater than that of the primitive man — certainly no greater than that of the ancient Sumerians or Greeks. Nor was it any less possible for Plato than it is for Einstein to make an ideal extension of his environment beyond the limits of immediate experience, or to conceive of a universe infinitely extended in space and without beginning or end in time. But the accumulated store of learning at the command of the modern man enables him to fill in the outer void of nature and history with more things and more familiar things — with stars and atoms of measurable mass and movement; with an endless succession of generations of men like himself, inspired with like motives, who brought to pass a series of related and credible events from remote times to the present. The ideally extended environment of the modern man is thus of the same texture as that of his immediate experience. Within this extended environment he can therefore move freely and without apprehension, so that however far he may wander in the outer void of nature or times past he finds himself at home because he meets with no alien men or strange inexplicable events.

It is this accumulated knowledge about the outer world of nature and the past history of mankind that places the modern man in a position to emancipate himself from bondage to ignorance and superstition, to subdue the physical world to his needs, and to shape his life in closer accord with the essential nature of men and things. Whether all this has been worth while, whether modern man is any happier than primitive man, whether modern civilization is superior or inferior to Greek civilization, may no doubt be debated. But it is beside the point. The point is that the impulse to know seems to be an inherent and ineradicable human trait. Since prehistoric times the impulse has persisted, and with every advance in knowledge the impulse has become stronger and more consciously directed. With or without the support or approval of established authority, by accident or in response to practical needs or as the result of deliberate purpose, the realm of verifiable matter-of-fact knowledge has been slowly enlarged, the realm of myth and insubstantial belief has been slowly restricted. Without any doubt this process will go on. Whether it makes us any happier or results in a better ordered world or not, it is our only resource. If we can find neither intelligence nor purpose in the universe at large, we must perforce rely upon our own. It is true that intelligence and purpose are not in themselves sufficient; they need to be restrained by integrity and good will. But integrity and good will are of little avail unless directed by intelligence, and the foundation of intelligence is knowledge — knowledge of what is true.

And so we arrive at our philosophical justification of freedom of learning and teaching — if you can call the justification philosophical. If we cannot justify freedom of the mind, and therefore freedom of learning and teaching, by saying that it is a God-given imprescriptible right, we can at least justify it by saying that the impulse to know what is true is an inherent human trait, that it has been the principal source of whatever happiness and ordered life man has been able to achieve, and that it is his only hope for a life better ordered and a happiness more general and more secure.

3

The practical justification of freedom of learning and teaching in a democracy is to be found in the fact that democratic government is self-government: in it the people de-

Freedom of Learning and Teaching

cide for themselves what shall be done to secure happiness and the well-ordered life, and it is obvious that they cannot make these momentous decisions to the best advantage unless the majority of them are intelligent and informed. That the majority may be intelligent and informed, that, as the Indiana constitution puts it, knowledge and learning may be generally diffused through the community, educational institutions are established — schools for the masses, colleges and universities for the leaders. It is commonly agreed that learning and teaching in schools and universities should be free in the sense that teachers should be free to teach and pupils to learn what is generally accepted by the community as true. But the practical question (always the difficult question) is what subjects should be taught, and just how free teachers should be to employ these subjects to indoctrinate pupils with ideas or theories that the majority of the people do not accept; theories that are still matters of dispute in the learned world and in any case may be no more than suggestive hypotheses rather than propositions capable of ever being proved either true or false.

This question does not arise in the primary or grade schools. No one denies that two and two equal four. The majority of the people would probably agree, at least if it were clearly pointed out to them, that "he has went" is not, strictly speaking, the preferred grammatical form. Nor is anyone, unless maybe the father of Huck Finn, likely to question the value of learning and teaching these useful truths. In high schools the question need not but sometimes does arise. The function of high schools is to teach immature minds what is known rather than to undertake the critical examination of the foundations of what is accepted in the hope of learning something new. What subjects should be taught is indeed a problem, and a difficult one; but whatever subjects may be chosen — mathematics, physics, biology, literature, history and civics, economics, me-

Freedom and Responsibility

chanical drawing, first aid, plain cooking, or the proper care of babies — the elements of what is definitely known about any of these subjects is sufficient, and could be taught, one might suppose, without serious offense to the morals and prejudices of the community.

One might suppose so, but in fact it cannot always be done. It depends in part on the discretion and common sense of the teacher, but chiefly on the intelligence and common sense of the people of the community — as, indeed, in the last analysis everything concerned with democracy does. During the last war, to take an example, an Iowa judge (I am sorry to have to say an Iowa judge, because I was born and brought up in that greatest of all states) announced publicly his considered opinion that American history and institutions, if taught at all in the schools, should always be taught in such a way as to demonstrate their obvious superiority to the history and institutions of all other countries. No doubt you will agree with me that this is nonsense. I hope you will agree with me that teachers should teach and pupils should learn, so far as possible, the essential facts of American history and institutions, and be allowed, like other citizens, to form their own opinions about the significance and value of that history and those institutions. But if the people of the great state of Iowa should agree with the Iowa judge (which they have not yet done), there is nothing anyone could do about it except to hope that the people of the great state of Iowa might in time become less hysterical and better informed.

Some years ago, to take another instance, the author of a high-school textbook on modern history was denounced in the newspapers as a Communist (that he was a well-known Communist could be proved, it was said, by "records in the Library of Congress") because he had set forth in his textbook the principal ideas of Karl Marx about history and society. That the ideas of Marx were correctly set forth was

Freedom of Learning and Teaching

not denied, but it was maintained that the author must share the ideas of Marx, since he did not denounce them. But the main point was that nothing at all, true or false, should be taught in high schools about Karl Marx, because Communist ideas were dangerous and high-school pupils might, if they learned what those ideas were, become infected with them. For similar reasons the teaching of the German language was forbidden in many schools during the last war. The logic of all this seems to be that it is all right for young people in a democracy to learn about any civilization or social theory that is not dangerous, but that they should remain entirely ignorant of any civilization or social theory that might be dangerous, on the ground that what you don't know can't hurt you. It is a weird species of logic in itself, and, what is more to the point, it is a complete denial of the democratic principle that the general diffusion of knowledge and learning through the community is essential to the preservation of free government.

Attempts such as these to interfere with freedom of teaching in high schools are deplorable, but it is easy to make too much of them. They are, if we take into account all the high schools and all the subjects taught, comparatively rare after all; and even these rare attempts are often enough inspired by other than the professed motives. The Iowa judge was probably less interested in the way American history should be taught than in showing that he was not to be outdone by anyone in patriotic hatred of the Hun. The protest against the teaching of Marxism was a local affair, and it turned out to be a political maneuver staged to discredit the superintendent of schools, who was a Republican, in the hope that some deserving Democrat might get his place.

But, aside from all that, it is a sound instinct on the part of parents to ask whether their children go to high school in order to be indoctrinated with interesting but debatable social theories. It must be remembered that high-school students are adolescents, and it is at least reasonable to maintain that the chief task of high-school teachers is to furnish the immature minds of their pupils with solid factual information. Whether the system of capitalist democracy is no more than a conditioned reflex induced by the factors of production is a fascinating and important question, but one may well doubt the ability of high-school students to arrive at any valid answer to the question, or even to discuss it intelligently, until they have learned what the factors of production are, besides a lot of other things. Nor is there much point in discussing with high-school students the meaning and significance of American history if they do not first know, for example, that California was not one of the original thirteen states, or that Washington did not deliver the Gettysburg address, or that the Gettysburg address was not a street number in Gettysburg where Lincoln once lived. That high-school students should learn something they or their parents do not know is admitted — admitted that they should be taught to think intelligently about what they learn. But by and large it may well be maintained that the primary task of the high-school teacher is to furnish immature minds with something solid to think about, rather than to present them with ready-made theories or interpretations of facts that they have not yet learned or cannot recall in their proper relations with any degree of accuracy.

If the general diffusion of knowledge and learning through a community is essential to the preservation of free government, then few things are more important than the sort of education that is provided in our high schools. But of the many and difficult problems that now confront high-school teachers and administrators, freedom of learning and teaching is by no means the most important. What subjects should be taught? Should all students be given essentially the same training, or should the students be provided with

Freedom of Learning and Teaching

quite different courses of study according to their native aptitudes and their prospective occupations? What can be done to prepare students for the responsibilities of citizenship? Above all, what can be done to confer on the teaching profession the prestige, the privileges, and the rewards that will attract to it men and women of first-rate ability?

These are some of the principal problems that arise in connection with high-school education. They arise also in connection with education in colleges and universities. But in colleges and universities freedom of learning and teaching, unhampered by the prevailing ideas and prejudices of the community, is fundamental, since without it colleges and universities lose their chief reason for existence.

Universities are commonly called centers of learning, and the origin of universities as we know them is commonly traced back to the twelfth century — to the parent universities of Paris and Bologna. But, disregarding names, the thing itself is much older. For the universities of Paris and Bologna were originally little more than groups of exceptional men surrounded by their pupils and engaged with them in the disinterested and systematic attempt to learn what is true. In a very real sense, therefore, the origin of universities as centers of learning carries us back to those exceptional individuals who first asked and attempted to answer all the fundamental questions about man and the world in which he finds himself.

One of the earliest, and perhaps the most famous, of these early centers of learning was established by Socrates at Athens in the fifth century B.C., and for the moment we may take it as an ideal or model university. It had no organization. It was limited to the essentials. It consisted of one professor and such students as he could beguile, at any time or place, to engage in discussing with him and with each other such questions as the meaning of virtue and justice, the nature of the gods, and what is essential to the good life. The

Freedom and Responsibility

value of this university was due entirely to the qualities of its professor, Socrates, who had the virtue that all professors should in some measure have — the virtue of being concerned above all things with the disinterested search for truth. The defect that professors and universities are prone to, Socrates managed to avoid: never, fortunately, having discovered any final truth, he was never in a position to rest on his laurels and abandon the search for it.

I am fully aware that this is an oversimplification of the virtues and defects of universities as we know them. The university of Socrates was a one-man affair, with relatively few commitments to the community. But universities as they have existed since the twelfth century have been institutionalized centers of learning, thoroughly warped into the social structure by their vested interests and loyalties, their traditions, and their rights and obligations as defined by the laws and customs of the land. Whether privately endowed or church- or state-controlled, they have always been explicitly or tacitly under bond to the community to provide for a select group of the rising generation what is called a "liberal education" — an education primarily designed to fit those who receive it for leadership in the community. Our own universities and colleges certainly devote the greater part of their endowment, their time, and their energies to what is called "teaching" rather than to what is called "research" — that is to say, to the transmission of what is known rather than to the critical examination of what is known and the expansion of the frontiers of knowledge. Nevertheless, the two functions of teaching and research cannot be divorced without loss to both. The education of college students for leadership in the community, if it be not constantly based on the results of current critical research, tends to become conventional and dogmatic and to leave the student with a body of information learned by rote and housed in a closed and incurious mind; while re-

Freedom of Learning and Teaching

search, carried on by professors secure in their tenure and under no obligation to concern themselves with the social significance of learning and teaching, tends to run into a barren antiquarianism, as harmless and diverting, and just about as socially useful, as cross-word puzzles or contract bridge.

In an ideal world the two functions of research and teaching would always supplement and reinforce each other: the new truth would always be immediately and painlessly assimilated to the old. In the world as it is the assimilation is always going on, but not always painlessly. There are always areas of danger — fields of knowledge and belief in which the new facts and the theories offered to explain them are apt to be regarded by the community as destructive of morality, vested interests, or public order. The classic example of this conflict is to be found in the trial of Socrates and the sentence of death inflicted upon him by the men of Athens because in their view his atheistical teachings were corrupting the youth of the city. The conflict symbolized by this famous event is perennial, and the community always holds the cup of hemlock, in one form or another, in reserve for those who teach too ardently or conspicuously facts or doctrines that are commonly regarded as a menace to the social order. The danger areas shift from time to time and from place to place, and the conflict may be more embittered and disastrous in one place or at one time than another. But in general it may be said that learning and teaching will be relatively free, and universities will for that reason be important centers for the advancement of knowledge, during those times when the political community and the fraternity of scholars are not in too flagrant disagreement in respect to the fundamentals of learning and the life of man.

This favorable situation exists either because the people do not know or take no interest in what is going on in the scholarly world, or because the political community (that is to say, those who control political action) have no sustaining convictions about morality and the good life, or because the basic assumptions of their political ideology are not essentially different from those accepted by scholars as essential for the promotion of knowledge. In fifth-century Greece the case of Socrates was exceptional. At that time scholars were for the most part free from political oppression; and apart from a peculiar conjunction of circumstances and personal animosities Socrates himself might well have lived out his life without molestation. During the Hellenic age scholars in the Alexandrian schools were mainly concerned with aspects of natural science or antiquarian historical research that had little bearing on politics or religion, and in any case they pursued their activities at a time when rulers and politicians were, either from skepticism or indifference, less inclined to attach importance to the ideas than to the utility of scholars. The Romans contributed little to the advancement of knowledge except in the realm of law and politics; and the Roman emperors, ruling over many and diverse peoples, were for reasons of political policy forced to be tolerant and to accept the view that all religions and ideologies were (in Gibbon's famous phrase) "considered by the people, as equally true; by the philosopher, as equally false; and by the magistrate, as equally useful." When the Christian philosophy of history and morality arose to threaten the basic conceptions of classical civilization the emperors attempted to suppress it; failing to do that, they adopted it as the state religion and closed the schools of Athens and Alexandria; and with the collapse of the Roman Empire knowledge and learning virtually disappeared in Western Europe until the revival of the eleventh century.

Mediaeval universities present us with an arresting paradox: they appear to us to have been singularly bound and

Freedom of Learning and Teaching

yet curiously free. We know that the mediaeval Church suppressed heresy with a ruthless hand, and yet nearly all the great scholars, from Abélard to William of Occam, were associated with some university sponsored by the Church and appear to have been quite free to learn what they could and to teach whatever they thought to be true. The key to this enigma is that at that time the common man, the constituted authorities, and the fraternity of scholars all accepted the Christian faith — the Christian story of man's origin and destiny — as the necessary basis of all knowledge and all ordered and virtuous living. The mediaeval scholar did not expect to find anything true that did not conform to the Christian story, any more than the modern scholar expects to find anything true that does not conform to the natural law of cause and effect. He could therefore contribute to the advancement of knowledge without offending the Church, because there was still plenty of room within the framework of the Christian story to learn again what the Greeks had known and the Arabs knew; and he felt no constraint so long as it was possible, by an ingenious use of logic, dialectic, and symbolism, to reconcile the new knowledge (new to Western Europe) with the Christian faith. After some two centuries, however, accumulated knowledge made the reconciliation of what was known with what must be believed too formidable, and the further advance of knowledge called for other premises and a different technique.

From the fifteenth to the eighteenth century other premises and a different technique were gradually adopted. The leading scholars turned from theology and philosophy to natural science and history; in place of logic and dialectic and symbolism they adopted the technique of observation, experiment, and the literal record of events; and in place of the Christian story of man's origin and destiny as the necessary premise in the search for truth, they accepted the modern conception of a universal natural law of cause and effect.

The result of all this was an unprecedented expansion of accumulated and verifiable knowledge — knowledge of the structure and behavior of the physical world and of the history of man's origin and activities. But the New Learning, except in so far as it was primarily antiquarian and without apparent bearing on the Christian story, could not be freely promoted in the established universities. The reason is that the Christian story was still accepted by the people as the foundation of the social order and the good life; the rulers of states, whether Protestant or Catholic, could maintain their power only by maintaining the religion acceptable to their subjects; and natural science and the interpretation of history, in so far as they denied, or were thought to deny, the validity of the Christian story, were therefore excluded from the universities altogether or admitted only with restrictions intended to make them innocuous. Of the thirty or forty leading scholars, from Erasmus to Gibbon, who rank highest in the history of learning, only a few were associated with any university, and of those few Kepler was driven out of Tübingen, Galileo was forced to recant his teachings, and Giordano Bruno, wandering from one university to another and welcomed in none, was finally burned at the stake. The scholars who contributed most to the advancement of knowledge were for the most part members of what Bayle called "the invisible college"; the visible colleges for the most part became, either through inertia or social compulsion, servile instruments of state policy, whose function, in effect if not in intention, was to support the authority of kings and defend the established religion.

This conflict between the political community and the fraternity of scholars was in theory ended, and in practice much abated, by the liberal-democratic revolution of the eighteenth and nineteenth centuries. The revolution was directed against the arbitrary authority of kings, the class privileges of nobles and priests, and the regimentation of opinion by church and state. In order to justify the revolution, political philosophers derived from the theory of natural law, which had long been accepted by scholars as the necessary premise in the search for truth, the natural and imprescriptible rights of men to the very liberties the revolution sought to win, and made these liberties the foundation of religion, morality, and public authority. In so far as the revolution succeeded, the old divergence between learning and politics was thus, in theory, ended. Both the political community and the fraternity of scholars professed to believe that the disinterested search for truth was essential to knowledge and the good life. Both professed to believe that the truth, so far from being something divinely revealed, was a progressive discovery negotiated by the open competition of individual judgments freely arrived at by the application of reason to the knowledge available. Both were therefore committed to the principle of freedom of learning and teaching, and by implication to the support of universities as places where the advancement of knowledge could be promoted without censorship or control by the state.

In theory the conflict was ended, but in practice the principle of freedom of learning and teaching enshrined in our political philosophy was not all at once, or ever completely, realized in administration of our colleges and universities. The ancient conflict between science and theology lingered on until science had contributed so much to business and to the convenience of the community that it was raised to the level of a religious faith. The conflict between vested interests and economic theory proved more enduring; and one must record the fact that, among those who made outstanding contributions to knowledge in the nineteenth century, Thorstein Veblen (to mention only one) was more or less

Freedom and Responsibility

politely elbowed out of academic centers of learning, and that many other men have found, and still find, their academic position precarious or untenable on account of their economic or political opinions.

I record the fact and deplore it. But if we compare the universities of Europe and America as they functioned in the nineteenth and early twentieth centuries, and as they still function in free countries, with the fate that has overtaken them in countries committed to an antidemocratic philosophy and practice, we cannot well miss the main point. The main point is that during the last three centuries there has been a close correlation between the spread of democratic government, the emancipation of the individual from restraints on freedom of learning and teaching, and the revival and expansion of colleges and universities as effective centers for the advancement of knowledge.

4

I have discussed, in separate categories, the philosophical and the practical justifications for freedom of learning and teaching. You may think that I have somewhat confused the categories. That may well be, for the philosophical and the practical reasons for freedom cannot really be separated, since they come to the same thing in the end.

In the last analysis democracy rests on the assumption that men have or may acquire sufficient intelligence and integrity to govern themselves better than any one or any few can do it for them — sufficient intelligence and integrity to manage their affairs with a minimum of compulsion, by free discussion and reasonable compromises voluntarily entered into and faithfully maintained. If this assumption is valid, then freedom of learning and teaching is essential, because it is obvious that the better informed the people are the more likely it is that the ends they desire will be wise and the measures taken to attain them effective. If the

Freedom of Learning and Teaching

assumption is not valid, or is not valid in the long run, then democracy is no more than a temporary phase — a luxury, as one may say, available only to those fortunate people who live in new and undeveloped countries, or countries endowed by peculiar and temporary circumstances with unaccustomed wealth, or small countries upon which nature or fortune have for the time being conferred some special felicities. In any case the only alternative to democracy is government by the one or by the few — government in which the many are subject to the will of the one or of the few; government in which it is for the one or the few to decide how much freedom of learning and teaching there shall be, how much the many shall be permitted to know, and what special mixture of truth and falsehood is best designed to keep them servile and contented.

For some years now we have been permitted, have indeed been forced, to contemplate and assess this unpalatable alternative. We have been told that democracy is no more than government by the few, no more than plutocracy, and that, having failed to provide for the welfare of the many, it is bound to be superseded by some more efficient system. We have seen these more efficient systems in action. We have seen, in Russia, the one-man and the one-party dictatorship suppress what little political freedom and freedom of opinion there may have been, and organize the economic life of the country without regard to the will of the people. We have seen, in Italy and Germany, the one-man and the one-party dictatorship, professing to represent the historic destiny of the nation or the right of the master race, embark on the conquest of Europe with a ruthless and scientifically calculated brutality and deception the like of which has never before been known. And we have been assured that this represents the "wave of the future" — a "new order" that will endure for a thousand years.

But we have seen something else — something that reassures us. We have seen this scientific systematization of force and fraud arouse first the loathing, then the fear, and at last the united resistance of the independent and the conquered and devastated nations of the world; and it is now clear that the new order that was to have lasted for a thousand years is already broken and will shortly be destroyed. Nevertheless, we need something more than superior force and military victory to assure us that democracy as we know it is not a passing phase — that democracy itself, in whatever altered form, represents the "wave of the future."

We may, I think, find some measure of assurance in the fact that democracy accepts in theory, and realizes in practice better than other forms of government, the humane and rational values of life, and that it is to that extent in harmony with the age-long human impulse to know that which is true and to follow that which is good — the impulse that throughout the ages, although often frustrated and sometimes defeated, has been the determining factor in lifting mankind above the life that, as Hobbes said, is "nasty, brutish and short." In all times past this inherent and indefeasible impulse has proved to be, with whatever reverses, the wave of the future; in the time that is before us, I think it will likewise prove to be, with whatever reverses, the wave of the future.

For the moment we are living in one of the periods of reverses, in a time when, as the poet Jeffers says, we seem to feel "a gathering in the air of something that hates humanity." Something that hates humanity and, for that reason, the truth too. The best case for democracy, and our best reason for having faith in the freedom of learning and teaching which it fosters, is that in the long history of civilization humanity has proved stronger than hate, and falsehood less enduring than truth.

IV
Constitutional Government

> We hold these truths to be self-evident; that all men are created equal; that they are endowed by their Creator with certain unalienable rights; that among these are life, liberty, and the pursuit of happiness; that to secure these rights, governments are instituted among men, deriving their just powers from the consent of the governed; that whenever any form of government becomes destructive of these ends, it is the right of the people to alter or to abolish it, and to institute new government, laying its foundation on such principles, and organizing its powers in such form as to them shall seem most likely to effect their safety and happiness.
>
> *The Declaration of Independence*

MODERN DEMOCRACY, as I have said, rests on the assumption that men have, or may acquire, sufficient intelligence and integrity to govern themselves better than any one or any few can do it for them. Political freedom is therefore inseparably bound up with freedom of speech and freedom of learning and teaching. But the term "political freedom" has acquired, in the United States at least, certain definite and limited meanings and connotations that make it desirable to discuss it separately. When it is said that the people of the United States enjoy political freedom we at once think of the rights we enjoy in respect to the creation and control of our Government — or governments, since we have many of them. In this restricted sense, political freedom, American style, means three things: first, that the people are the sole source of all political power; secondly, that the form of government is republican; and thirdly, that the powers of government and the rights of citizens

Freedom and Responsibility

are defined in fundamental organic laws called constitutions.

When the first constitutions were adopted it was taken for granted that the form of government would be republican — that is, government by representatives elected by the people. It was also taken for granted that the people are the source of all political authority. In the Declaration of Independence Jefferson expressed the doctrine of the sovereignty of the people in the terse phrase: "Governments are instituted among men, deriving their just authority from the consent of the governed." The same doctrine, variously worded, is set forth in all our state constitutions; nowhere better, perhaps, than in the Texas Constitution of 1845: "All political power is inherent in the people, and all free governments are founded on their authority and instituted for their benefit; and they have, at all times, the unalienable right to alter, reform, or abolish their form of government, in such manner as they may think expedient." Just who comprise the people in this sense (whether the people of the several states or the people of the United States) was long and bitterly disputed, and a civil war had to be fought to decide the issue. But the main point is that, since 1789 at least, we have always taken it for granted that the people, however defined, have at all times the right to alter, reform, or abolish their form of government in whatever way and to whatever extent they may think necessary or desirable.

That the people are the sole source of political power is thus essential to our conception of political freedom. But it is by no means the whole of it. "The people" comprise many people — many individuals with diverse and conflicting interests and wills; and in a republican form of government the only practicable way to reconcile this conflict of wills, of determining in any specific case the will of the people, is by majority vote. Jefferson accepted majority vote as a necessary practical device, but he was not so naïve as to

Constitutional Government

suppose that the majority would be always right or never unjust. His contemporaries agreed with him, and on the whole the people of the United States have always agreed with him. Of necessity we trust the people as a whole, as they proceed by majority vote to alter, reform, or abolish their form of government in such manner as they may think expedient. But as individuals, impatient of restraints on our freedom to say and do what we like, we are a little afraid of the people as a whole; and accordingly we have always taken precautions against hasty or ill-considered action on their part. We have, as one may say, appealed from the people drunk with the possession of political power to the people sobered by the fear of political oppression. And the interesting and significant result is that, although no nation is more entirely committed than we are to republican government operating by majority vote, we have found more (and more ingenious) ways of moderating, delaying, sidestepping, and hamstringing the will of the majority than any other nation has thought it necessary or desirable to submit to.

The over-all device for safeguarding the rights of individuals and the interests of minorities against the hasty or ill-considered will of the majority is the system of written constitutions, Federal and state. We are so familiar with this system that it seems to us in no way extraordinary. With us it goes without saying that we must have written constitutions, and that the ones we have are in all essentials entirely satisfactory. But it is no bad thing, every now and then, to examine what goes without saying in order to see whether it is still going. It will be worth while, therefore, to examine our system of written constitutions in order to see what they were originally designed to do and whether and how effectively they are still doing it.

Freedom and Responsibility

2

The idea of a written constitution is an old one, being little more than the adaptation of private contract to the organization of public relations; but the idea acquired high prestige in the eighteenth century because of the widespread belief that society could be deliberately and advantageously reconstructed according to a rational plan. The founding fathers of the American Republic were not entirely uninfluenced by this optimistic idea, but the constitutions they drafted were shaped far less by political theory than by historical experience and precedent. Such rights of self-government as the colonies had were defined in their respective colonial charters; and in the perennial disputes between colonial assemblies and royal governors, and later between the assemblies and the British government, the colonial leaders constantly appealed to the charters as organic acts guaranteeing their rights of self-government.

The colonial charters thus became, with some assistance from political philosophy, the prototypes of the state constitutions. When the colonies separated from Great Britain eleven of the thirteen sovereign states adopted new constitutions that were scarcely more than revised editions of their colonial charters, while the other two, Rhode Island and Connecticut, retained their charters as organic constitutions without any revision at all. For fighting the War for Independence a political union of the thirteen states was obviously necessary, and this union called for a federal constitution — first the abortive Articles of Confederation, and then the more perfect union created by the Constitution of 1789. Subsequently, as new states were admitted to the Union, the people of each state as a matter of course adopted a constitution for that state essentially similar to those with which they were familiar. There are now forty-eight states, and some of them have from time to time as-

Constitutional Government

sembled constitutional conventions and adopted new constitutions in place of the old.

The French historian Taine made a great ado over the fact that the French people had, within less than a hundred years after 1789, adopted as many as thirteen constitutions. No American would think that anything to write home about. Taine should have looked into Benjamin Perley Poore's collection, in two massive volumes, of the American constitutions. There he would have found that within a hundred years after 1776 the people of the United States had adopted one hundred and four constitutions, with no assurance that the business would end there. That would no doubt have seemed to Taine astounding and incredible, but we think nothing of it. We think nothing of it chiefly because, in making a new constitution, we have never, since 1789, really had to think at all. All we have ever had to do is to copy, with some modifications in detail, the model created by the founding fathers — that is to say, a document which sets forth the natural and inalienable rights of the citizen and provides for the organization of another republican government of the stereotyped pattern in which the powers of government are dispersed among magistrates, separated in respect to function, and otherwise rendered innocuous by applying the grand negative principle of checks and balances. In reading any of our state constitutions one finds oneself suddenly transported into the eighteenth-century climate of opinion, contemplating political ideas and devices admirably suited to sustain the faith of the founding fathers in the sovereignty of the people, and at the same time to abate their lively apprehension as to what might happen to political freedom if the people were permitted, except on rare and solemn occasions, to exercise that sovereignty without restraint.

The occasions on which the sovereignty of the people can be exercised without restraint — on which, as one may say,

Freedom and Responsibility

the will of the majority is effectively unleashed — occur only when the people are willing or can be induced to assemble constitutional conventions. In normal times the will of the majority can be effective only within those absolute limitations and through the intricately channeled procedures defined in the constitutions already established.

The absolute limitations on governmental action are set forth in the bills of rights. Governments exist, as the Declaration of Independence has it, in order to secure the natural rights of man. But Jefferson and his contemporaries regarded some of these rights as of such fundamental importance to the individual that they should never be abolished or infringed by any government, even a republican government. In all our constitutions, accordingly, we find these rights declared to be imprescriptible, and therefore placed above and beyond the reach of legislative or administrative action. They are the so-called civil liberties.

We are all supposed to know our civil liberties as well as we know the multiplication table; but just in case some of them have slipped our memories it will be worth while to set them forth in precise legal language. For this purpose we might choose any of the state constitutions, but the present occasion makes it appropriate to choose the Constitution of Michigan. The civil liberties, as defined in the present Constitution of Michigan (as amended to 1936), may, with some rearrangement in order and some slight omissions, be presented under the following five heads:

1. *Religious freedom.* Every person shall be at liberty to worship God according to the dictates of his own conscience. No person shall be compelled to attend, or, against his consent, to contribute to the erection or support of any place of religious worship, or to pay tithes, taxes or other rates for the support of any minister of the Gospel or teacher of religion. No money shall be appropriated or drawn from the treasury for the benefit of any religious sect or society, theological or religious semi-

nary; nor shall property belonging to the state be appropriated for any such purpose. The civil and political rights, privileges and capacities of no person shall be diminished or enlarged on account of his religious belief. No person shall be rendered incompetent to be a witness on account of his opinions on matters of religious belief.

2. *Freedom of speech.* Every person may freely speak, write and publish his sentiments on all subjects, being responsible for the abuse of such right; and no law shall be passed to restrain or abridge the liberty of speech or of the press. In all prosecutions for libels the truth may be given in evidence to the jury; and, if it shall appear to the jury that the matter charged as libelous is true and was published with good motives and for justifiable ends, the accused shall be acquitted. The people shall have the right peaceably to assemble, to consult for the common good, to instruct their representatives and to petition the legislature for redress of grievances.

3. *Rights in respect to trial and punishment.* The right of trial by jury shall remain, but shall be deemed to be waived in all civil cases unless demanded by one of the parties in such manner as shall be prescribed by law. In every criminal prosecution, the accused shall have the right to a speedy and public trial by an impartial jury; . . . to be informed of the nature of the accusation; to be confronted with the witnesses against him; to have compulsory process for obtaining witnesses in his favor; to have the assistance of counsel for his defense. . . . No person shall be compelled in any criminal case to be a witness against himself, nor be deprived of life, liberty or property, without due process of law. No person, after acquittal upon the merits, shall be tried for the same offense. All persons shall, before conviction, be bailable by sufficient sureties, except for murder and treason when the proof is evident or the presumption great. The privilege of the writ of habeas corpus shall not be suspended unless in case of rebellion or invasion the public safety may require it. Treason against the state shall consist only in levying war against it or in adhering to its enemies, giving them aid and comfort. No person shall be convicted of treason unless upon the testimony of two witnesses to the same overt act, or on

confession in open court. No bill of attainder, ex post facto law or law impairing the obligation of contracts shall be passed. Excessive bail shall not be required; excessive fines shall not be imposed; cruel or unusual penalties shall not be inflicted; nor shall witnesses be unreasonably detained. Any suitor in any court . . . shall have the right to prosecute or defend his suit, either in his own proper person or by an attorney or agent of his choice. No person shall be compelled in any criminal case to be a witness against himself, nor be deprived of life, liberty or property, without due process of law.

4. *Security of persons and possessions.* Neither slavery nor involuntary servitude, unless for the punishment of crime, shall ever be tolerated in this state. The person, houses, papers and possessions of every person shall be secure from unreasonable searches and seizures. No warrant to search any place or to seize any person or things shall issue without describing them, nor without probable cause, supported by oath or affirmation. . . . No person shall be imprisoned for debt arising out of . . . a contract, express or implied, except in cases of fraud or breaches of trust.

5. *Security against military power.* Every person has the right to bear arms for the defense of himself and the state. The military shall in all cases and at all times be in strict subordination to the civil power. No soldier shall, in time of peace, be quartered in any house without the consent of the owner or occupant, nor in time of war, except in a manner prescribed by law. No person shall be imprisoned for a military fine in time of peace.

Such are the civil liberties as set forth in the Constitution of Michigan. They are similarly set forth, with minor differences in form or content, in all our constitutions; and the purpose of thus setting them forth is to define a sphere of action that is entirely withdrawn from governmental control.

But even within the sphere of action in which the government has authority, the power of the government to act is limited in many ways. The liberal-democratic revolution of

Constitutional Government

the eighteenth century was directed against a social system in which political power was excessive, arbitrary, and concentrated. The founding fathers were therefore predisposed, both by political experience and the political philosophy they embraced, to regard political power as inherently dangerous; and to their way of thinking the essential purpose of a written constitution was to devise a system of government in which political power would cease to be excessive and arbitrary by being strictly limited in scope, and would cease to be concentrated by being dispersed, checked, and balanced in its application.

I need not say that the founding fathers were eminently successful in attaining this object. In the form of government which they devised, and which in all essentials still exists, political power is dispersed first of all between the Federal and the state governments according to the principle that "the powers not delegated to the United States by the Constitution, nor prohibited by it to the States, are reserved to the States respectively, or to the people." Within the Federal Government, and within each of the state governments, political power is further dispersed, according to the eighteenth-century principle of "separation of powers," among the legislative, executive, and judicial branches of the government; and on the chance that any of these branches might acquire too much power within its own domain, each branch is further hampered by permitting the others to check its action in certain circumstances. Thus the executive cannot make laws, but it can veto those made by the legislature. The legislature cannot execute laws, but it can refuse to appropriate the money needed for that purpose. The courts can neither make laws nor execute them, but they can declare a law made and executed null and void if in their judgment it violates the Constitution. These are the principal but by no means the only ways in which political power is checked and balanced in our system of gov-

Freedom and Responsibility

ernment. In the Federal Government especially there are other refinements — so many that we may and often do achieve an equilibrium of political power so balanced and buttressed that movement backward or forward is imperceptible because virtually nonexistent. In a system of government so competently designed to safeguard the rights of individuals and the interests of minorities, the tyranny of the majority is indeed a remote contingency.

Such was the system of government created by the founding fathers. In the course of a hundred and fifty years some changes have inevitably been made in it. The Federal Constitution has been amended several times and unamended once. It has been battered by circumstances and stretched by interpretation to give the Federal Government far more extensive powers than the founding fathers anticipated or would have thought desirable. The method of electing the president has been by common consent so far changed that the procedure now followed is, in spirit if not in form, a violation of the Constitution. But in its structure and operation the American system of federated governments is essentially what the founding fathers made it. It is the American contribution to political science, and that it is an outstanding contribution is not to be denied. Probably no system of government, unless it be the English, ever solved more successfully the fundamental problem of politics — the problem of the one and the many: of reconciling the desirable liberties of the citizen with the necessary powers of society; of conferring on local communities the maximum of self-government without enfeebling the state; of recognizing the will of the majority and at the same time placing checks on hasty or ill-considered action. Nevertheless, admirable as the American system of government is, and partly because it is so admirable, we need to be reminded that a system of government designed to meet the problems of the eighteenth century is not necessarily in all respects suited to meet the problems of the twentieth.

We need to be reminded of this more especially because we are rather too apt to regard our constitutions as sacred tables handed down from Mount Sinai — documents revealing those fundamental principles of government which, being universally applicable, need never be re-examined. It is as if in the eighteenth century we discovered and labeled our liberties, locked them safely away in oak-ribbed and riveted constitutions, placed the key under the mat, and then went cheerfully about our private affairs with a feeling of complete security. From time immemorial men have been eager to believe that political authority is divinely ordained; and our constitutions provide us with compensation, as one may say, for loss of faith in the divine right of kings by assuring us that our system of government is in accord with the eternal laws of nature and of nature's God. We commonly think and speak of our liberties as "constitutional liberties," and on the whole we speak of them a great deal without thinking about them very much. The constitutions give us a feeling of safety and relieve us of the sense of responsibility. We feel that our civil liberties are safe because they are enumerated in the constitutions, and that our political freedom is safe because the government is so bitted and bridled and hobbled that it can't run away with the wagon however loosely we hold the reins. We feel safe because, the fundamentals having been settled once for all, we feel that we have a foolproof and enduring government — in short, a government of laws and not of men.

Ours is indeed a government of laws — forty-nine constitutions and more statutes than can be easily mastered by the human mind; and if it be a government of laws and not of men, why indeed should we not divest ourselves of responsibility and put it all on the laws, since there are so many of them? In normal times, when nothing of great mo-

Freedom and Responsibility

ment troubles us, we are therefore disposed to take politics lightly, as an exciting, even a rough and somewhat sordid game, played with gusto and hullabaloo according to accepted rules, in which nothing of much importance is at stake except the satisfaction of winning. If the game becomes a bit too rough, we can change the rules. If our conscience is troubled by what men do, our first instinct is to say: "There ought to be a law against it." We expect to purify politics by laws limiting campaign expenses; to make a nation of gamblers prudent by laws against betting; and to make a nation of hard drinkers temperate by amending the Constitution. In more critical times, when profound moral issues arise to threaten our comfort or security, we still count on the laws to see us through; being confident, for example, that we can avoid the Nazi menace by keeping out of war, that we can keep out of war by remaining neutral, and that we can remain neutral by enacting a statute — a law of neutrality, a law of cash-and-carry. Having a government of laws, and so many laws, makes us a legally minded people, predisposed to think that adherence to the letter of the law, if only we can be sure the law is constitutional, is sufficient for salvation.

This attitude of mind was never better disclosed than during the controversy occasioned by the conflict between North and South prior to the Civil War. The issue that threatened and finally dissolved the Union was the institution of chattel slavery. After 1830 the institution of slavery, becoming every year more offensive to the moral sense of the nation and of the world, could no longer be considered to any good purpose merely in terms of economics and legality. The only effective solution short of war was voluntary emancipation of the slaves by the Southern states and compensation for the slave-owners by the Federal Government. Yet few people on either side, except the Abolitionists, were willing to admit that slavery need be regarded as more than a local institution like any other — a "peculiar institution" perhaps, but one clearly sanctioned by the Constitution and the laws of the land. At no time did this legalistic approach to the slavery question reach a higher degree of refinement than in the enactment of the Compromise of 1850. When passions ran so high that a doorkeeper in the House of Representatives could not be chosen without making sure that his attitude to the peculiar institution would be equally satisfactory to all of those who could not themselves agree on the subject, it was manifestly impossible for either side to make concessions of any practical value. The Compromise of 1850 was, therefore, a futile effort to put an end to an "irrepressible conflict" over a profound moral issue by making concessions to wounded pride, lost prestige, and constitutional rights — concessions that conferred no advantage. It is not strange, then, that the Compromise of 1850 turned out to be in effect to be the compromise that ended all compromises.

We are now living in another critical period of our history. The house is again in the way of being divided. The division is not now between people living in different sections of the country, but between people living on different social levels in respect to possessions and opportunities. But the division, now as then, is occasioned by divergent ideas about human rights and property interests. There are those who profess to believe that when the war is over this conflict can be composed by returning to something called the American system of free enterprise which they like to think existed before 1933. I do not share that optimism. We are not only engaged in a world war, but also we are involved in a world revolution. Whatever the outcome of the war and the nature of the peace we cannot return, even in this fortunate country, to the old happy-go-lucky attitude that during most of our history has served well enough — the habit of regarding economics as a realm apart, in which the best man wins and devil take the hindmost; of regarding politics as a national sport staged periodically by politicians to decide who shall have the places; of regarding civil liberties and political freedom as negotiable securities of high and enduring value because they are locked away in written constitutions.

In this critical time we shall not keep the house united and preserve our liberties by refusing to recognize that economics and politics are not separable from ethics and morality, or by Seventh-of-March speeches advising the people not to discuss the institution of private enterprise, which is in fact the central issue. Above all we shall not preserve our freedoms by resting in the comfortable conviction that they are secure because defined in the constitutions. To revere the founding fathers is all very well, but it would be better if we followed their example by re-examining the fundamental human rights and the economic and political institutions best suited to secure them. And perhaps the first step in that direction would be to open up our eighteenth-century constitutions in order to see whether the civil liberties as therein defined, and the form of government as therein organized, are in all respects suited to the complex conditions of our time and the complicated problems that in fact confront us. If we should do that, certain important questions would inevitably arise. I can do no more than indicate what some of them are.

3

Take first the civil liberties. All of these (with the possible exception of the right to bear arms, which seems now advantageous chiefly to gangsters) are, in respect to the end contemplated, invaluable and should be preserved; but one may well ask whether they are defined in the bills of rights with sufficient care to attain the end desired in the complex social conditions of the modern world.

Constitutional Government

The right of the people to assemble and consult for the public good is exercised with little let or hindrance: we still have our town halls, social forums, and campaign speeches. But where the people chiefly assemble is in front of their radios to consult with disembodied voices that announce and comment on the news collected by corporations organized for private profit. The right of assembly is a part of the right of free speech and of the press; and in our time the practical problem has to do, not so much with those who may freely assemble and speak their minds, but rather with those who may acquire a virtual monopoly of collecting and disseminating information. Freedom of speech is of little use to those who have not free access to the principal means of communication; and nothing in the bills of rights is of much help in determining whether freedom of speech and of the press is maintained or denied by the Associated Press and the broadcasting corporations.

Moreover, freedom to print is useless if it does not include the right to circulate what is printed. Not long ago the editor of the *Saturday Review of Literature* was advised in a letter from the postmaster of the New York City post office that the book *Strange Fruit* was not mailable, and that if the *Review* continued to print advertisements of that book it would run the risk of being itself excluded from the mails. The editor of the *Review*, getting in touch with the post office by telephone, was informed by an assistant that the postmaster, although his name was signed to the letter, had neither written nor seen the letter — it was a mere matter of routine. When the editor suggested that freedom of the press seemed to him rather too important to be settled as a mere matter of routine, the assistant replied: "All right, so you say this is very important to you. Well, Mister, it's only a small detail to us." Freedom of the press is guaranteed by the Federal Constitution and in the Constitution of New York; but surely it is not adequately defined in

Freedom and Responsibility

those constitutions if it permits an impudent clerk in the New York City post office to be entrusted by law with what amounts to a censorship of the press.

The right of a citizen charged with crime to a fair and speedy trial is likewise an invaluable right; but it is relevant to ask whether the judicial process as now conducted is the best method of securing that right. The trial of Lawrence Dennis and other persons charged with sedition may have been fair, but it was certainly not speedy. In the course of centuries complicated technical rules of evidence and of procedure have been developed, many of them originally designed to protect ordinary citizens against the arbitrary procedure of a tyrannical government. Now these technicalities are often employed by skillful but unscrupulous attorneys to drag out cases and befuddle issues in defense of persons known to be guilty, or to exclude evidence, because it was obtained under an improper form that might prove the defendant guilty if it were admitted. All citizens are guaranteed against arbitrary arrest and imprisonment and against cruel and unusual punishments. This right is sustained by the courts when cases involving it are brought before them, as in the recent United States Supreme Court case *Ex parte Mitsuye Endo* concerning the retention of Japanese-American citizens in relocation centers. But the right is not secure merely because defined in our bills of rights and sustained by the courts, since every day citizens are "detained for questioning" by the police (whose activities are in effect, if not in theory, parts of the judicial process) and, if they refuse to answer on the ground that they are not charged with crime, are likely, if they be not "persons of prominence," to be subjected to the third degree on the assumption that the truth can be elicited by torture if the torture be sufficiently painful and prolonged.

Of all our civil liberties, few are more celebrated than the right of a person charged with crime to a trial by a jury of his peers. The right was established in England at a time when it was thought that the neighbors of a man accused of crime would know more about the circumstances of the crime and the persons involved in it than anyone else, and could therefore render a more just judgment. Today the prime qualification for service on a jury is complete ignorance of the circumstances of the crime and of the persons involved in it. Jury trial in criminal cases has become a carefully staged combat between two sets of skilled attorneys, each set primarily concerned, not with establishing the truth about the crime, but with limiting and distorting the evidence in the way best calculated, on the one side to convince the jury that the defendant is guilty, on the other to convince the jury that he is innocent. The function of the judge is to see that the rules of law are observed. The function of the jury is supposed to be to determine the facts. But it is obvious that the ordinary jury is quite incapable of determining the relevant facts elicited in a long and complicated trial, even if they had the full record before them and sufficient time to examine it thoroughly. This is so well understood that in some states judges are now permitted, by their comments on the evidence, to relieve the jury of an impossible task. Where that is not possible, it is scarcely too much to say that the real task of the jury is to guess, with such aid as it can, by questions, induce the judge to give, which set of attorneys has been the most adroit in confusing the witnesses and clouding the issue.

Not that any particular blame attaches to attorneys. No more than other people do they really wish to convict an innocent or discharge a guilty defendant. They are prisoners of the system. Better than anyone they know that juries are incapable of performing the function assigned to them. In many states the right to be tried by a jury may now be waived by the defendant, and is rather often so waived. If jury trial works even tolerably well in states where it is

Freedom and Responsibility

compulsory, the chief reason is that by and large the legal profession is composed of men of intelligence and integrity who do the best they can, within the limitations of the system, to prevent a miscarriage of justice. It is the system that is defective; and its fundamental defect is that it proceeds on the assumption that if, within the rules of evidence, the facts are distorted twice but in opposite directions, the truth will emerge and justice will be done.

We are so familiar with trial by jury in criminal cases that it is difficult to look at it objectively. Besides, we have been taught to believe that the administration of justice in English and American courts is the best that has been developed in any society. Taken by and large, that is true. But it still remains true that trial by jury, as a method of determining facts, is antiquated, unscientific, and inherently absurd — so much so that no lawyer, judge, scholar, prescription clerk, cook, or mechanic in a garage would ever think for a moment of employing that method for determining the facts in any situation that concerned him. I am far from suggesting that the judicial process, or any part of it, should be lightly abandoned, or even reformed without the most careful consideration. But certainly in this age, when fact-finding has become very nearly an exact science, some better method could be devised for determining the guilt or innocence of a person accused of crime than one that excludes much relevant evidence, makes far too much of whatever distinction there may be between "direct" and "circumstantial" evidence, and turns the investigation over to two sets of rival attorneys whose professional success depends, not on finding out what happened, but on winning the case.

It is obvious that the bills of rights could be rephrased in such a way as to secure our civil liberties more effectively, and on first thought that might seem the obvious and wise thing to do. The difficulty is that we have forty-nine bills

Constitutional Government

of rights, and if any substantial change, either in content or form, is made in one of them, essentially the same change should be made simultaneously in all of the rest; otherwise our civil liberties might vary from state to state as much as our divorce laws do, and come to be regarded with the same levity and derision. It is probably a sound instinct on the part of the people to feel that it is dangerous to meddle with our bills of rights. But it is equally dangerous to feel that our civil liberties are secure because they are constitutionally guaranteed. If the civil liberties, or some of them, are denied every day to someone, and few people bother about it unless they are directly concerned, and most of us feel that those who do bother about it must for that reason be Jews, Reds, or crackpots — if that is the way we take it (and by and large it is), then less than nothing is gained by reflection that our civil liberties are secure because they are abstractly defined in the same archaic phraseology in forty-nine bills of rights and may be defended in as many courts of law.

If reverence for the bills of rights obscures the fact that our civil liberties are not so secure as we think, worship of a constitutional system of government that has worked so well for so long a time tends to blind us to its manifest defects.

The virtues of our system of federated governments are indeed very great. Its chief virtue is its capacity to maintain political unity in a large country of diversified interests and ideas without imposing uniformity of political organization and administrative procedure upon it. It confers extensive powers of local self-government on the states, permits local experiments in the solution of political and social problems, and at the same time maintains a high degree of political unity among a hundred and thirty-eight million people spread out over a vast continent. It does this through the system of federated governments, the method of electing governors, state legislatures, and members of Congress, and not least through the election of the president by a majority of the electoral votes — a complicated system of elections which makes it virtually impossible for any political party that is organized primarily on sectional or class lines to obtain control of the Federal Government. For this reason there are (and one might almost say there can be) only two political parties strong enough to have any chance whatever of winning a national election. For this reason the two major parties differ very little in the fundamental principles they profess or the policies they advocate. The chief difference between them is that one is in, or mainly in, and wishes to keep in, while the other is out, or mainly out, and wishes to get entirely in. In a national election neither party, whether in or out, can afford to adopt a program that is radically different from that adopted by the other, because both parties must appeal to many sections and all classes and to both conservative and progressive opinion. The most that either party can do is to shift the emphasis a little for or against progressive or conservative policies, be more or less skillful in writing a platform that is all things to all men, rely upon the popularity or ability of its candidate (if he has either), and then make a dead set to carry the doubtful states. If the party that was out gets in, it can't do anything very radical or revolutionary. No more than the party it has displaced can it afford to alienate any major interest in any part of the country by moving from the middle of the road too far to Right or to Left. The system is thus a conserving, stabilizing, unifying force. It calls for compromise (for "appeasement," if you want a bad word), for softpedaling the things that divide the people and emphasizing the things that unite them.

These are very great merits. But the defects of our system of government are obvious and were long ago clearly pointed out. One of the principal defects is its inflexibility.

Constitutional Government

It responds to the calendar rather than to the course of events. Seven-score and sixteen years ago it was foreordained that there should be a presidential election in the year 1944. If the political situation should make it unnecessary or undesirable to hold an election at that time, so much the worse for the political situation. Once elected, a president, no matter how inefficient he may be or how completely he may have lost the support of the people, cannot, except by a major operation known as impeachment, be got rid of until four years have passed. As Woodrow Wilson acidly remarked, a British prime minister, in order to retain office, must "keep himself in favor with the majority, a President need only keep alive." There is no elastic element, as Walter Bagehot pointed out in his penetrating analysis of the Federal Constitution. "Every thing is rigid, specified, dated. Come what may, you can quicken nothing and can retard nothing. You have bespoken your government in advance, and whether it suits you or not, whether it works well or ill, whether it is what you want or not, by law you must keep it." You must keep it at least for four years; and in the meantime whatever important issue arises, however desirable it would be to refer it at once to the people for decision, cannot be so referred until the first Tuesday after the first Monday in November of the proper year rolls around.

But the most striking defect of our system of government is that it divides political power and thereby conceals political responsibility. The business of governing is entrusted to the President and the Congress, but it too often happens that no body of elected representatives can be held responsible or called to account for the formulation of policies or the enactment of measures to carry them through. The President can recommend policies, but the Congress can reject them. The Congress can formulate policies only indirectly by passing specific measures, but the President can

Freedom and Responsibility

veto any or all such measures. If they are nevertheless passed over his veto, he is faced with the choice of carrying out measures of which he does not approve or by indirection sabotaging their execution.

The system works well enough only on those rare occasions when a political party, winning an election hands down, is united and can count on strong popular support. This occurred in 1932, and again in 1936. But since then, as a result of discontent in the country and disaffection within the party, the President virtually lost control of Congress to an opposition composed of Republicans and conservative Democrats. And the result is that now, in the midst of a desperately fought war and at a time when we need to make crucial decisions about postwar reconstruction, the situation is such that neither the President nor the Congress nor the political party in power can be held clearly responsible, separately or conjointly, for what is done or not done. On the contrary, we have been and may still be forced to contemplate the unedifying spectacle of the White House and Capitol Hill working at cross-purposes, pursuing different and perhaps conflicting policies, and at worst indulging in mutual recrimination or engaging through the newspapers in a competitive struggle for popular support.

In other countries — notably in France and the South American republics — governments similar to or modeled upon that of the United States have often enough in times of crisis broken down. That the system has worked as well as it has in the United States is due partly to the political sense and self-restraint of the people and partly to the fact that times of crisis have been rare. But it is extremely unlikely that the easy conditions that have prevailed in the past will continue; and for dealing with the difficult national and international problems that confront us it would be well if we had a form of government in which political power and political responsibility were more conjoined,

Constitutional Government

more clearly defined and definitely placed, and more responsive to the popular will.

The direct and deliberate way to make the needed change is by a revision of the Federal Constitution. This would be an extremely difficult thing to do at any time, and is in any case to all intents and purposes impossible at the present time. Not that it is very difficult, although it requires time, to amend the Constitution if the people really want it amended. When the people wanted national prohibition, the Constitution was amended without much trouble; when they got tired of prohibition, it was unamended with even less. But amending the Constitution in matters of detail is one thing; a revision of its basic structure is quite another. So far no amendment has touched the principle of separation of powers which is fundamental in the structure of all of our governments; and at present there is no effective demand for any modification of the principle of separation of powers, or even any widespread realization that it is not essential to the preservation of political freedom. I believe, nevertheless, that sooner or later some modification of that principle will have to be made: if it be not made deliberately, it will be made by indirection or default. I doubt very much whether, in a world loaded with social dynamite, we can go on forever muddling through with a system of government so admirably adapted for passing the buck and debasing the business of governing to the level of personal squabbles and party intrigue.

To suppose that our civil and political liberties are secure because they are abstractly defined in written constitutions is to mistake the legal form for the living substance of freedom. It is desirable, it is indeed necessary, to have a government of laws; but to suppose that because we have a government of laws we have not a government of men is a misleading and dangerous fallacy. No government, even a government of laws the most wisely conceived and effectively ordered, can ever be better than the people who administer and submit to it; and in a republic if the people, either through ignorance, indifference, or dishonesty, renounce responsibility for the preservation of their freedom, the laws, whether constitutional or statutory, will not preserve it for them.

V
Private Economic Enterprise

> Marx was the first to see . . . that the evolution of private capitalism with its free market had been a precondition for the evolution of all our democratic freedoms. It never occurred to him . . . that if this was so, these other freedoms might disappear with the abolition of the free market.
>
> *Max Eastman*

THE LIBERAL-DEMOCRATIC revolution, as I have said, was directed against those forms of government in which political power was excessive, concentrated, and arbitrary. For this reason it proceeded on the assumption that a proper system would provide for a minimum of governmental authority and a maximum of individual liberty. The liberties that could be demanded with the most assurance and denied with the least grace were the liberties of person and opinion — freedom of religion, freedom of speech and of the press, freedom from arbitrary government, freedom from the insane brutalities practiced in the civil and ecclesiastical administration of justice and the punishment of crimes. These were the freedoms that all men could understand and from which all could benefit. There was, however, another freedom, less stressed by philosophers and less important for purposes of revolutionary propaganda, which became an essential part of the revolutionary program. This was the right of private economic enterprise.

This right is not mentioned in the American bills of rights as one of the natural and inalienable rights of man. The reason may be that it was already so well established and so little denied that it could be taken for granted. The

Freedom and Responsibility

right is, however, implied in those provisions that guarantee the individual against unwarranted seizure of his possessions and against the confiscation of private property for a public purpose except by due process of law and for an adequate compensation. The right of private economic enterprise is inseparable from the right of private property, and both are closely associated with equality of status and the right of individuals to choose their occupations. In most countries before the Revolution the status of individuals was relatively fixed, the right to choose one's occupation was greatly restricted, and both industrial and commercial enterprises were carefully regulated by law on the mercantilist theory that governmental control of the economic life of the community was essential to increase the available wealth of the country by maintaining a "favorable balance of trade." For these reasons the leaders of the French Revolution could not take the institution of private property or the right of private economic enterprise for granted. Various decrees were passed establishing equality of status. In the Declaration of the Rights of Man and the Citizen, property is specifically included among the natural and inalienable rights of man; and the decree of March 2, 1791, which abolished the industrial guilds, laid down the general principle that "every person shall be free to engage in such business, or to practise such profession, art or craft as he shall find profitable."

Thus the right of private property and of free private economic enterprise, whether taken for granted as in the United States, or made explicit as in France, became one of the essential liberties associated with the liberal-democratic revolution. The right was in accord with the current political philosophy, but it was more explicitly formulated in the writings of the French economists of the eighteenth century, in Adam Smith's *Wealth of Nations,* published in 1776, and in the more rigorous and ostensibly more scien-

Private Economic Enterprise

tific writings of the English classical economists of the early nineteenth century.

For describing the economic theory thus formulated the words "laissez faire" came into common use. The laissez-faire theory (which might be rendered the "let-alone" or "hands-off" theory) was primarily an economic theory, but by implication a political theory as well. In respect to politics, it maintained that the government should confine its activities to the preservation of life and property, the enforcement of private contracts, the maintenance of civil order, and the protection of the country against foreign aggression. In respect to economics it maintained that the individual should be free to choose his own profession or business and to enter into private contracts for the acquisition and disposal of property and for the purchase and sale of personal services. As an economic as well as a political philosophy it rested on the current doctrine of natural law. It assumed that the best results would be obtained for the life of the community if men were left as free as possible to follow their natural instincts and aptitudes. The free play of individual initiative, stimulated by the natural acquisitive instinct, would result in the maximum production of wealth, and the natural competitive instinct, operating through the law of supply and demand and the resulting price system, would result in as equitable a distribution of wealth as the natural capacities of men would permit.

It is now obvious that the laissez-faire theory was scarcely more than a rationalization of the economic interests of middle-class business men and promoters, and that it had little to commend it from the point of view of the working masses and their interests. But that ominous fact was long obscured because the theory was formulated in terms of the magic word "liberty." The average humane middle-class man, whether a business man and an employer of labor or not, could easily accept freedom of economic enterprise

Freedom and Responsibility

along with all the other great freedoms, since it so happily enabled him to reconcile his selfish with his altruistic instincts and relieved him of responsibility for his unfortunate brother man by assuring him that he could best serve God and his neighbor by doing as he pleased. "Private profit a public advantage" — such was the succinct formula that enabled so many men of intelligence and good will to entertain the comfortable belief that the pursuit of individual interest would result automatically in a harmony of interests, so that if every man looked out for himself without regard to others the devil would after all not take the hindmost, because something not himself, God or Nature, would do whatever else was necessary for righteousness.

In the nineteenth century, in those countries where liberal-democratic governments were established, the laissez-faire doctrine was widely accepted and more or less applied in practice. In no country was the theory more commonly accepted or more fully applied than in the United States; in no country were the conditions such as to make the virtues of the system more apparent or its evils less disastrous. For the average man in all countries, and perhaps especially in the United States, the refinements of the theory were neither understood nor regarded as important; it was enough to know that government should never "meddle in business." This idea became so firmly entrenched that to this day it is the settled conviction of many, perhaps most, business men in the United States; and they believe sincerely that in so far as government does now regulate private business enterprise it has departed from some earlier and happier time when government did not meddle, and private enterprise was perfectly free.

The fact is, of course, that there never was such a time. Private economic enterprise could be perfectly free only in some imagined state of nature in which no government existed. Whenever in any society there is a government that

Private Economic Enterprise

guarantees private property, enforces private contracts, and maintains civil order, there is a government that meddles in business by placing restraints on the freedom of the individual in economic enterprise. The laissez-faire theory itself provided for such meddling and such restraints; and accordingly, both from the theoretical and the practical point of view, the relevant question now and always has been, not whether government should meddle in business by placing restraints on private economic enterprise, but just how much meddling it should do and just what restraints it is necessary or desirable to apply.

The answer to this question now depends, as it always has depended, on the concrete situation, and the concrete situation varies from country to country and from time to time. In the eighteenth and early nineteenth century the laissez-faire theory was a sound working principle for emancipating industry from the hampering restraints of monopolistic privilege and petty governmental regulations. But, applied without qualification, it necessarily worked to the benefit of the industrial middle class at the expense of the underlying population of agricultural and industrial workers. Even under the most favorable conditions a society of uprooted and freely competing individuals must have functioned to the advantage of the few who by good fortune, intelligence, or lack of scruple were able to acquire wealth and to employ it to advance their interests through the mechanism of politics: the times would always be ripe for a sufficient number of not-too-good men to come to the aid of the party. But this result was greatly accelerated and intensified by those changes in the economic and material conditions of life which, effected without blare of trumpets and scarcely noted at the time, are now known as the industrial or the technological revolution of modern times.

Technological is the better word. The word "industrial" is quite inadequate to denote one of the two or three major revolutions that have occurred in the history of the race. Man is a tool-using animal, and all civilizations have been conditioned by the sources of natural power known to him and by the mechanical appliances he has been able to invent to make such power available for use. The first great epoch of discovery and invention takes us back before the time of recorded history. All the more obvious sources of natural power — gravitation, fire, wind and water, domestic animals, the fertility of the soil — and the simple hand tools and appliances for making these sources of power available were known to primitive man. Since the invention of writing, some four or five thousand years ago, few new sources of natural power were discovered until comparatively recent times; and the mechanical appliances available, although they became far more numerous and much perfected, remained essentially of the same order as those used from time immemorial.

But we are now living in the second great epoch of discovery and invention. Since the seventeenth century the discovery of steam power, gas, electricity, and radiation has made possible all of those powerful machines, tools, gadgets, and instruments of precision that elicit our wonder and our admiration. The result has been the new technology, which, by giving men unprecedented control over material things, has transformed the relatively simple agricultural societies of the eighteenth century into societies far more complex, impersonal, and highly integrated than anything the prophets of liberal democracy could have imagined — into those mechanized Leviathans which Thomas Jefferson, at least, would have regarded as unreal, fantastic, and entirely unsuited to the realization of liberty and equality as he understood these terms.

At all events, in these complex and highly integrated societies the theory of laissez faire — according to which government would not meddle in business, and the pro-

Private Economic Enterprise

duction and distribution of wealth would be effected by free competition and the flexible response of the price of goods and of labor to the natural law of supply and demand — proved quite inadequate. On the contrary, in every country in which the new technology was adopted, and more or less in the measure that it was developed, there appeared a disturbing paradox — a paradox indicated by Henry George in the title of his famous book, *Progress and Poverty*. The paradox was this: that whereas the system of private economic enterprise, employing the new technology, was capable of an enormous increase in the production of wealth, it proved incapable of making an equitable distribution of it. Progress in the production of wealth marched side by side with widespread poverty; in countries capable of producing plenty, millions were destitute.

The most general result of this situation, as it has developed during the last hundred years, has been to demonstrate with increasing clarity that the laissez-faire theory was based on false or at least inadequate assumptions and could not be realized in practice in any industrialized country without disastrous social consequences. In every industrialized democratic country it has been found necessary, in order to correct the manifest evils of private economic enterprise, for the government to "meddle in business" more and more; and this meddling has been commonly justified on the assumption that the proper function of government, so far from being confined to the preservation of life and property, the enforcement of contracts, and the maintenance of civil order, is to do whatever may be necessary to provide reasonably decent conditions of living for the people as a whole.

2

To denote this general trend away from the theory and practice of laissez faire, two expressions have lately come to be widely used. One of them is "collectivism." The other is "managed economy." In this country the word "collectivism" has a bad odor because most people identify it with the word "communism." The term "managed economy" smells almost as bad. I have no great attachment to particular words and am quite willing to use any word, or even the letter X, just so an agreed-upon meaning can be attached to whatever word or symbol may be thought best. The important thing is the set of historical facts or events which the word or symbol represents; and whether we use the words "collectivism," "managed economy," "governmental regulation," or the letter X, the historical fact is that during the last hundred years there have emerged various forms of collectivism, managed economy, governmental regulation, or X, differing partly in respect to the extent of regulation or control they advocate, and partly in respect to the means they propose for effecting such regulation or control. These different forms of X we might call Alpha, Beta, Gamma, and Pi. Let us, however, call them Socialism, Communism, Fascism, and, for want of a better term, Social Democracy.

The trend towards what I have called Social Democracy appeared first in England, the first country to become industrialized by applying the new technology. In England the abandonment of the old mercantile system is commonly said to have been completed by the repeal of the Corn Laws in 1846; but it is significant that more than a decade before the laissez-faire theory was thus officially accepted, the evils of the system, as exhibited in the cotton mills, were already so ghastly that it was found necessary to restrict freedom of contract in the employment of children. The first of the so-called "factory acts," passed in 1833, prohibited the employment in factories of children under nine years of age, limited the hours of labor for children between nine and thirteen to forty-eight hours a week, and of

Private Economic Enterprise

children between thirteen and eighteen to sixty-nine hours a week! Since this was an improvement, we can imagine what the original situation must have been.

But the main point is that this was the first of the "factory acts"; and since that time the British Parliament has passed an increasing number of laws placing restraints on private economic enterprise, all designed to provide a greater degree of equality of possessions and of opportunities between the rich and the poor. Similar legislation for a similar purpose has been enacted in all democratic industrialized countries. Such legislation has been commonly called "social legislation," or "social reform"; its purpose has been to achieve social as well as political democracy; and it has been justified, tacitly if not explicitly, on the assumption that it is a proper function of government to regulate private economic enterprise in so far as may be necessary to aid the less fortunate classes of society at the expense of the more fortunate classes.

To this general rule the United States is no exception. I have said that in no country was the theory of laissez faire more commonly accepted or more generally applied in practice than in the United States, and so far as the regulation of particular business enterprises is concerned this is true enough. But it would be a mistake to suppose that the people of the United States have ever really doubted that it is a proper function of government to promote the general welfare. Although Americans have commonly believed that government should never meddle in business, no class of Americans, so far as I know, has ever objected (such is the inconsistency of the human mind) to any amount of governmental meddling if it appeared to benefit that particular class. Since 1815 the Federal Government has regularly enacted tariff laws ostensibly designed to protect infant industries, maintain a high standard of living for labor, and sustain the price of agricultural products. The Federal

Freedom and Responsibility

Government has constructed highways, has given public lands to railroads, and subsidies to steamship companies. Millions of acres of public land have been set aside as an endowment for schools and universities, and most states have maintained at public expense free schools mainly for the benefit of the poorer classes. In 1862 the Federal Government passed the Homestead Act, which permitted any head of a family or citizen twenty-one years of age to acquire one hundred and sixty acres of public land virtually free of cost if he would live on that land for five years. Few people notice the little vans that run about the streets collecting mail, but they are parts of one of the largest business enterprises in the country — a business enterprise owned and operated with exceptional efficiency by the Federal Government. No one thinks that the United States Post Office is a menace to private economic enterprise; and if the government had built, owned, and operated railroads and telegraph lines from the beginning no one would now think that it was meddling in business.

All these measures and activities were in contravention of the theory of laissez faire. All were based on the assumption that it is a proper function of government to limit the individual initiative of some people and to assist the initiative of others. All were based on the assumption that it is a proper function of government to do what the Federal Constitution was designed to do — "to promote the general welfare."

Nevertheless, the regulation of particular enterprises, which is what Americans commonly think of as government meddling in business, began in the United States at a comparatively late date. In the third quarter of the nineteenth century farmers complained that the railroads were charging them excessive or discriminatory rates for transporting farm products. In 1873 certain Western states passed laws regulating freight rates, and the courts sustained these laws

Private Economic Enterprise

on the ground that "the State must be permitted to pass such rules and regulations as may be necessary for promoting the general welfare of the people."

This decision may be taken as the official denial, casual as it may have been, of the theory of laissez faire and the doctrine that government must never meddle in business. At all events, from that time to the present many laws have been passed, by the Federal and by the state governments, placing restraints of one sort or another on the activities of business corporations, all designed to protect the people against the evil effects of private economic enterprise. Many people profess to believe that the so-called New Deal of the present administration is something brand new and revolutionary — a complete reversal of our traditional custom, something that denies in theory and tends to destroy in practice the American system of free economic enterprise. In fact it was nothing new, but merely a revival and an extension of measures for social reform that Theodore Roosevelt called the "Square Deal" and Woodrow Wilson called the "New Freedom." Particular measures of the New Deal may have been well or ill designed to effect the end desired; but the New Deal itself was in harmony, both in theory and in practice, with the long-established American tradition that the state "must be permitted to pass such rules and regulations as may be necessary for promoting the general welfare of the people."

It is, then, an obvious historical fact that during the last hundred years there has been, in every democratic industrialized country, including the United States, an increasing amount of governmental regulation of private economic enterprise. The object of such regulation has been to correct the manifest evils of free competition by bringing about a greater degree of equality of possessions and of opportunity for the mass of the people. The method by which it has been effected has been the method of discussion, compromise, and legislation by the democratic procedure. This regulation of economic life by the democratic governments is the form of collectivism or managed economy that I have called Social Democracy. It rests on the assumption that it is desirable to preserve the capitalist system of private enterprise, and that the evils of this system can be sufficiently corrected by the democratic method of procedure.

Nevertheless, during the last hundred years there have been many who have denied this assumption, who have asserted on the contrary that the capitalist system of free enterprise for private profit is itself the chief cause of social injustice, and that accordingly all attempts to correct the evils of the system while preserving the system are bound to fail in the end. Other forms of collectivism or managed economy have therefore been proposed or adopted. These are known as Socialism, Communism, and Fascism.

Socialism and Communism in their modern forms derive from the philosophy of history and economic theory formulated by Karl Marx in the mid-nineteenth century. The Marxian philosophy (which Marx called communism or "scientific socialism," to distinguish it from other forms of socialism) rests on the assumption that the structure and transformation of society are fundamentally determined by impersonal economic forces rather than by the wills and aspirations of men. In the Middle Ages, for example, land was the most important form of wealth, the landowning aristocracy was therefore the ruling class, and the prevailing social and moral customs and ideas were those best suited to maintain the power and prestige of that class. But when in the course of some centuries wealth in the form of capital became more important than land, the bourgeois-capitalist class which controlled this new form of wealth elbowed the feudal landowning aristocracy out of the seats of power and adopted those liberal-democratic institutions (representative government, freedom of speech and reli-

Private Economic Enterprise

gion, freedom of private economic enterprise) which were better suited to promote its interests and maintain its power. This transfer of economic power from the feudal landed aristocracy to the bourgeois-capitalist class was, according to Marx, the essence of what is called the liberal-democratic revolution of the eighteenth and nineteenth centuries: the liberal-democratic ideology was merely, as he might have said, accessory after the fact — a reasoned justification of the forcible usurpation of political control by the class which the shift in economic influence had made the dominant class.

Marx did not deny that the capitalist-democratic revolution was an important and necessary stage in historical progress. It abolished many evils, established many liberties, made possible the rapid advance in scientific knowledge and technology, and thereby resulted in an enormous increase in the production of wealth. But society is not static; and according to the Marxian doctrine the democratic-capitalist system, although a necessary stage in the dialectic of history, was a temporary form, bound, like the feudal system before it, to be transcended by something better. It would be transcended, not by wishing or by argument or by denouncing its evils, but by its own inherent economic "contradictions." Free private economic enterprise and ruthless competition would inevitably concentrate wealth in the hands of the few most intelligent and unscrupulous capitalists and gradually reduce the mass of the people (the proletariat) to the level of a bare subsistence. When this inevitable and irreversible process was sufficiently matured, business expansion would slow down because more goods could be produced than the impoverished proletariat could buy, and a series of increasingly severe economic depressions would end in economic and political disintegration. Then the proletariat, made desperate by its miseries, conscious of its rights, and instructed in the Marxian philosophy of social revolution, would establish a temporary dictatorship of the proletariat, confiscate private property in land and industry, liquidate the capitalist classes, and after the revolution was accomplished establish a classless society and a truly democratic government which would organize the production and distribution of wealth for the common good.

In the late nineteenth century this doctrine of inevitable social revolution was widely accepted by the industrial workers in most European countries. While waiting for the coming revolution, which could neither be much advanced nor retarded by anything men could do, the workers formed socialist political parties, elected representatives to the legislative bodies in the various countries, and advocated advanced egalitarian programs of social reform. But ten years after the death of Marx in 1883 many of the prophecies of Marx seemed falsified by events, and the revolution seemed a long time coming. For this and other reasons the socialist political parties split into two groups — the majority and the minority parties. The minority parties still adhered to the orthodox Marxian doctrine of revolution by collapse and violence, but the majority parties accepted a "revised" Marxian doctrine which maintained that the social revolution (the abolition of the capitalist system of private economic enterprise for private profit) could be achieved without violence — by the education of the people, the triumph of the socialist parties at the elections, and the consequent nationalization of land and industry through the constitutional democratic procedure.

During the early years of World War I both parties lost prestige and power; but the Russian Revolution of October 1917 gave a spectacular and world-wide significance to the orthodox Marxian doctrine of revolution by violence. To characterize the form of socialism established in Russia and to distinguish it from the "revisionist" forms advocated by

Private Economic Enterprise

the majority socialist parties in other European countries, Lenin used the word "communism." Since the Russian Revolution, therefore, Communism and Socialism have usually meant quite different things to those who belong to the communist and socialist parties in Europe and America. They agree in believing that the capitalist system of private enterprise for private profit is the major source of social injustice and must be abolished; but whereas the socialists think that this can be done within the framework of democratic government and by peaceful democratic procedure, the communists maintain that it can be done only by violent revolution, dictatorship, and the forcible liquidation of the capitalist classes. The difference, although ostensibly a difference in method only, is a radical one. It is the difference between those who believe that the democratic form of government and the democratic political and intellectual liberties can and should be preserved, and those who believe that, temporarily at least, they can and must be destroyed.

Social Democracy, Socialism, Communism — these are the three forms of collectivism or managed economy that emerged in the nineteenth century. There is a fourth form which goes by the name of Fascism. The roots of the Fascist tree run deep into the nineteenth century, but the tree itself sprang up suddenly and unexpectedly after World War I. According to the Marxian philosophy the social revolution would occur first in the most highly industrialized country (England probably), and then spread rapidly to other industrialized countries. In fact it occurred first in Russia, one of the least highly industrialized countries of Europe, and did not spread to any major industrial country. Revolutions occurred (in Italy, Germany, Spain, and other countries), but so far from being communist they were in part inspired by fear of Russian Communism. For all that, however, there are certain similarities between

Freedom and Responsibility

Italian and German Fascism and Russian Communism. All three systems were established by violent revolution. All three were one-man and one-party dictatorships. All three suppressed the democratic liberties as we understand them; and in all three (although in Italy and Germany land and industry were not as in Russia formally nationalized) the economic life of the community was so completely controlled by the government that private enterprise for private profit as we understand it virtually disappeared. Nevertheless, the differences between Fascism and Communism as exhibited in Germany and Russia are important. Communism rests upon a reasoned philosophy of history and politics that was propagated for fifty years before it was established in Russia. Fascism was scarcely more than an invention of Mussolini and Hitler to serve their personal ambitions, and it is supported by a philosophy, if you can call it that, hastily devised after the event. Taking the two philosophies as standards for judging the two systems, the differences are radical. Communism is democratic — that is, the dictatorship is regarded as temporary, a necessary device for carrying through the revolution, to be replaced ultimately by a government of, by, and for the people: Fascism is antidemocratic — the dictatorship and the suppression of individual liberties are regarded as permanent. Communism is international — it preaches the brotherhood of man and the equality of nations; Fascism is anti-international — it denies the equality of nations as well as the equality of individuals, and preaches the supremacy of the nation or of the master race. Communism is pro-intellectual — it declares that social progress rests on knowledge, and that knowledge can be attained only by the disinterested search for truth; Fascism is anti-intellectual — it regards science and the search for truth as of no importance except in so far as they can be used for the attainment of immediate political ends.

Private Economic Enterprise

It will be said that in Russia the ideals of Communism are not in fact lived up to. That is true. It is also true that the ideals of democracy are not lived up to in the United States, England, or any other democratic country. The ideal forms that, according to Plato, are laid up in Heaven, rarely correspond with much exactness to their earthly counterparts. But the ideal forms are not to be despised or lost sight of for all that. The political philosophy, the set of values, which any form of government professes and attempts to live up to is of vast importance. The worst thing that can be said about the Americans or the English or the Russians is that they do not live up to their ideal aims. The worst thing that can be said about the German Nazis is that they do live up, or down, to their ideal aims. They suppress the truth and practice brutality, not merely as temporary means for the attainment of ends that cannot for the time being be otherwise attained, but deliberately, systematically, and with malice prepense as permanent means inseparable from ultimate ends and having in themselves the same inherent virtues.

3

These are the four forms of collectivism or managed economy that have emerged during the last one hundred years. They are alike in one respect only: they all reflect the trend in all modern industrialized societies towards a greater degree of governmental regulation of the economic life of the community. In other respects they differ more or less radically. What are the essential differences?

We can make the essential differences clear by defining briefly the traditional democratic liberties and then asking what part of these liberties the four forms of collectivism require us to give up. The traditional democratic liberties can be briefly defined under three heads. First, intellectual liberties — freedom of speech and of the press, of religion, of learning and teaching. Second, political liberties — free discussion of public affairs, free election by the people of government officials, and the enactment of such laws as the elected representatives can agree upon and the people will support. Third, economic liberties — the right of private property and of private economic enterprise for private profit. Social Democracy asks us to give up none of these liberties, but only to submit to such governmental regulation of private economic enterprise as may be necessary to correct its evils and secure a reasonable degree of equality of possessions and of opportunities for the mass of the people. Socialism asks us to give up permanently the right of private economic enterprise for private profit, but assures us that none of the other liberties need ever be surrendered. Communism asks us to give up permanently the right of private economic enterprise for private profit and the intellectual and political liberties as well for the time being, but allows us to hope that the one-man and one-party dictatorship will at some uncertain future time find it expedient to restore them to us. Fascism asks us to give up all of our liberties forever and to trust to the one-man and one-party dictatorship to think and to act for us better than we can think and act for ourselves.

Which of these four forms of collectivism or managed economy do we want? No doubt the great majority of the people in the United States would reply: "We do not want any form of collectivism at all." In most cases I think the reply would be instinctive, inspired by aversion to the word "collectivism" more than by the thing itself. But there is really no use in saying we do not want any form of collectivism or managed economy, in the sense that I am using these words — no use, that is, in saying we do not want any sort of governmental regulation of private economic enterprise. We already have a good deal of it; and it is about as certain as anything can be that we shall have more. To say that we do not want any form of governmental regulation of eco-

Private Economic Enterprise

nomic life is like saying that we should be better off without Diesel engines, automobiles, airplanes, and broadcasting stations. Maybe we should. But we have these things, we cannot get rid of them by wishing, and while we can adjust our lives to them in one way or another, it is mere folly to suppose that we can refuse to adjust our lives to them in any way whatever.

When I was a boy there was almost unlimited individual initiative and free private enterprise in driving on the highway. The only rules of the road were two: if you met anyone driving in the opposite direction, you turned to the right; if you wished to pass anyone driving in the same direction, you turned to the left. Now the rules of the road are many and complicated. Traffic lights and traffic cops, signs to slow down or to stop, arrows indicating which streets are one-way streets and in which direction the one way is — these are obvious indications that individual initiative and free private enterprise in driving on the streets and highways have been subjected to a great deal of governmental regulation. No one in his senses thinks that such regulations, or some regulations of a similar nature, are not necessary. But this is only one instance of the general fact that the complex nature and the rapid tempo of technological society have made the trend towards governmental regulation of economic and social life necessary and therefore inevitable. We cannot reverse that trend, but we can, by taking thought, determine within limits the nature and extent of such regulation. We can choose whether we will have the kind of governmental regulation that I have called Social Democracy rather than the kinds I have called Socialism, Communism, and Fascism.

We can choose, but maybe any choice we make will prove futile. It is possible that the economic and social contradictions arising in the modern world are no more than superficial symptoms of a discord more profound — the discord

Freedom and Responsibility

between the physical power at our disposal and our capacity to make a good use of it. Long ago it was said that it is easier for man to take a city than to govern himself. Never was that saying more true than now. Never before has the intelligence of men placed so much material power at their disposal; never before have they used their power for the realization of purposes more diverse or more irreconcilable. The machines we have invented seem often enough to enslave us by generating, before we are aware, those social forces which, being too complex and intangible to be easily understood, shape our lives to ends we do not will but cannot avoid. It is, then, within the range of possibility that the flagrant discord between the material power at man's disposal and his capacity to make a good use of it is carrying the world into another period of widespread and chronic confusion in which democracy will everywhere succumb to dictatorship, reason to naked force, and naked force prove the prelude to another dark age of ignorance and barbarism.

I do not think this will happen. I feel, indeed, quite sure it will not happen. But it is futile to think that it cannot happen, futile to rely upon something not ourselves (a law of nature or dialectic of history, forms of government and bills of rights defined in written constitutions, an abstraction called free economic enterprise) to bring us in spite of ourselves to some predestined good end. If we come to any good end we must get there by our own efforts; and the off-chance that our efforts may all prove futile does not relieve us of the responsibility of choosing what we want and trying to obtain it. It need not be said that we (the vast majority of the people of the United States) do not want either Communism or Fascism. Almost as little do we want Socialism. But it does need to be said that if we let things drift we are in danger of getting the form of collectivism or managed economy we want least. We cannot easily drift

Private Economic Enterprise

into Communism or Socialism or Social Democracy. If we let things drift, the thing we are the most likely to drift into is Fascism.

Fascism is more dangerous than Communism for many reasons. One is that we fear it less. We are deluded by the notion that the military defeat and destruction of a few gangster governments in the countries where Fascism has triumphed will eliminate the conditions favorable to the rise of Fascist governments in any country. Another reason is that Fascism is not bound up with any elaborate and consistent philosophy of history and politics, but rests on a few ideas and impulses that are native in every country — national egoism, race prejudice, the natural impulse of average men to revere and follow a leader. Latent in every country, these ideas and impulses easily become dominant in a country that is disintegrated by economic insecurity, bitter class conflicts, and loss of faith in the principles and efficiency of the existing form of government. Under these circumstances Fascism appeals to ignorant and defeated men, to cynical and disillusioned men, to corrupt men on the make, and to all who place too high a value on political authority and too low a value on political liberty.

The conditions that might lead to some American brand of Fascism would be those created by another Great Depression more disastrous and prolonged than the last one: twenty million men out of jobs and without hope for the future; farmers with crops rotting on the ground and no remedy in sight except to limit the production of foodstuffs; labor unions discredited by gangster tactics and businessmen in a mood to "smash the unions" at all costs; class conflicts too embittered to be reconciled and pressure politics too unrestrained to be joked about; a "bundles for Congress" movement sweeping the country. Such a situation, if sufficiently prolonged, might bring to life the deep-seated conviction of the average American that confusion and in-

Freedom and Responsibility

justice are not things to be taken lying down, might release his ingrained impulse to, and his native capacity for, direct action. The movement, whatever form it might take, would not be known as Fascism, still less as Nazism. It would be heralded by some native American slogan, such as "efficiency for freedom" or "the national cleanup"; and whatever form it might take, it would still be known as the American way of life.

If we would eliminate the conditions that might lead to some American brand of Fascism, we must give at least as much intelligent and disinterested attention to the achievement of Social Democracy as we are now giving to the winning of the war. The problem is easily stated: how to maintain the maximum production of wealth and get it properly distributed among the people. The experience of the last fifteen years presents this problem in the form of a paradox: whereas before the war all our efforts to maintain full production and avoid mass unemployment met with an indifferent success, as soon as we became fully involved in the war these evils disappeared. This was also the experience of all capitalist democratic countries that entered the war. The relevant question stares us in the face. Is war the only means available to capitalist democratic countries for curing business stagnation and mass unemployment? In order to cure one serious evil is it necessary to become involved in another and worse one? If so, then we might as well say good-by to the capitalist system and our democratic liberties. If not, the only condition on which we can preserve the capitalist system and our democratic liberties is to find some means other than war for making the capitalist system work in the United States, and to do what we can to get rid of war altogether as a means of settling the inevitable conflicts that arise between nations.

This problem cannot be solved by letting things ride. It cannot be solved by bombarding each other in the dark

Private Economic Enterprise

with jet-propelled phrases, such as "bureaucracy," "states' rights," "mature economy," "the American Way of Life," and the like. Nor can it be solved by playing politics — by calling the prewar depression a "Hoover Depression" or a "Roosevelt Depression" and thinking that all will be made right by putting one political party in power rather than another. The problem cannot be solved without a good deal of governmental aid and supervision. But neither can it be solved by a series of unco-ordinated measures, each one designed to cure some specific evil without regard to the others. Nor can it be solved by any measures designed primarily to place restraints on productive enterprise — limiting the production of cotton and wheat in order to raise farm prices, spreading out and slowing down the work in order to raise the wages of labor, and then freezing prices and wages in order to prevent inflation. Still less can it be solved by supplanting private economic enterprise by a centralized governmental organization and direction of economic life — an organization that, like an engineer's blueprint, purports to take account of all contingencies and to foresee the finished structure.

I, at least, am one of those who believe that if we cannot preserve a very large measure of individual initiative and private enterprise for private profit, it will be exceedingly difficult to preserve that degree of intellectual and political freedom without which democracy cannot exist. I think, therefore, that the primary aim of all governmental regulation of the economic life of the community should be, not to supplant the system of private economic enterprise, but to make it work.

The system of private economic enterprise for private profit works well only when there are adequate opportunities and incentives for business expansion. The war now provides these opportunities and incentives, and as a consequence business stagnation and mass unemployment have disappeared. When the war is over opportunities for expansion will be found in what can be sold abroad and in what the people of the United States need and can pay for. What they can pay for is, of course, the rub. What they need can be easily stated — more food, clothes, houses; the abolition of slums and the rebuilding of a hundred or more cities to make them decent and convenient places to live and work in; more and better parks, playgrounds, recreation centers, art galleries, and theaters; the expansion and co-ordination of all systems of transportation; the expansion of schools and universities and facilities for adult education; the building, equipping, and staffing of more and better hospitals, asylums for the mentally defective, and centers for medical and other scientific research. The list of things needed for improving the national welfare could be indefinitely extended. We all know this, and it is obvious that if we could be as united, determined, and ingenious in devising and carrying through a nation-wide program of social improvement as we have been in devising and carrying through a program for winning the war, we could forget about business stagnation and mass unemployment.

You will perhaps say that the If is a big one. It is indeed. It is so much easier to unite for avoiding an immediate and understood common danger than for the attainment of a remote and disputed common good. The fundamental question, no doubt, is whether the private-profit motive can be sufficiently reconciled with the common desire for the general welfare. If it cannot, we are in for a bad time. Apart from some such program for social welfare that will provide for the expansion of business enterprise and thus win the support of the people (that is to say, the farmers, businessmen, and labor), there seems nothing in sight but a return to the policies and limited successes of the New Deal, or something essentially similar — mistaking symptoms for causes, giving subsidies to businessmen and farmers to keep them going, giving relief checks to the destitute to keep them alive. Something better than that is needed if we are to have, after the war is over, the sixty million jobs and a national income of a hundred and fifty billion dollars that are said to be essential.

One thing that is needed in this country is an abatement of the traditional feeling of enmity between business and government — the feeling that in so far as government intervenes in the economic life of the community, private enterprise must be curtailed. According to Geoffrey Crowther,[1] the British, who have much the same tradition, have been forced by the pressure of events to take a different view — a view expressed, as he thinks, by two prominent Englishmen. "Mr. Oliver Lyttelton, a conservative," says Mr. Crowther, "remarked . . . that if anyone asked him whether the country needed more state organization or more free private enterprise, his answer would be that it needed a great deal more of both. And Mr. Herbert Morrison, a socialist, . . . said that there is a case for private enterprise and a case for public enterprise, but no case at all for private or public unenterprise." Mr. Crowther quotes these men in support of the conclusion that in England all parties are agreed that in order to save private enterprise they must have more of it, and that in order to have more of it there must be intelligent co-operation between government and business.

The essential point for us is, not to imitate the British, but to recognize that the proper function of government in the present situation is not to hamper business but aid it. So long as governmental measures for regulating the economic life of the community are designed primarily to place restraints on the expansion of private enterprise, or at any rate have that effect, they will fail to attain the end desired. They will fail because the majority of the people

[1] *The Yale Review*, XXXIV, 222.

Freedom and Responsibility

(businessmen, farmers, labor) will oppose them, and they will fail in any case because the end desired is increased production and you cannot get increased production by laws placing restraints on productive enterprise. The essential thing, then, is for business and government (the people and their elected representatives) to cease sniping at each other, abandon the attitude of an armed truce, and endeavor to learn (and both have much to learn) what the situation is exactly, and precisely what measures on the part of the government will in fact remove the obstacles that now stand in the way of business expansion and thereby bring about full production and employment.

Fortunately, there is now before Congress a bill which indicates that this is perhaps not too much to hope for. The bill in question is the Murray-Kilgore bill, first introduced in 1944, but reintroduced on January 22, 1945, by Senator Murray on behalf of himself and Senators Wagner, Thomas (Utah), and O'Mahoney, and referred to the Committee on Banking and Currency. (Senate Bill S. 380, first session, 79th Congress)

This bill (to be cited as "Full Employment Act of 1945"), whatever its defects may be, has the great merit of proceeding on a sound general assumption. The assumption is that the proper way to deal with economic depression is not to wait until it becomes too serious to be ignored and then trump up some hastily devised and unrelated measures to cure it, but to provide in good time the measures that will prevent it from becoming serious. The object of the bill, in short, is "to establish a national policy and program for assuring a *continuing full employment* in a free competitive economy, through the concerted efforts of industry, agriculture, labor, State and local governments, and the Federal Government."

The provisions of the bill are presented under four main heads: (1) Declaration of Policy; (2) The National Pro-

Private Economic Enterprise

duction and Employment Budget (to be referred to as the National Budget); (3) Preparation of the National Budget; and (4) Joint Committee on the National Budget.

Not the least interesting and significant part of the bill is the declaration of policy. It is the policy of the United States (1) "to foster free competitive enterprise . . . in developing the natural resources of the United States"; (2) to recognize the "right" of all Americans able and willing to work to "useful, remunerative, regular, and full-time employment"; and (3) to "ensure at all times the existence of sufficient employment opportunities to enable all Americans . . . freely to exercise that right." Furthermore, in order to carry out these policies "it is the responsibility of the Federal Government to pursue consistent . . . economic policies and programs" that will, first of all, stimulate private enterprise and other non-Federal investments and expenditures; and if that proves inadequate, "it is the further responsibility of the Federal Government to provide such volume of Federal investments and expenditures as may be needed to assure continuing full employment." More simply, if there are sixty million Americans able and willing to work, then there must be sixty million jobs provided for them. If the jobs can be provided by private enterprise, well and good. If not, then the Federal Government must aid private enterprise in expanding its investments and expenditures, and if that is not sufficient to provide the jobs, then the Federal Government must make investments and expenditures of its own to take up the slack.

Such being the responsibility of the Federal Government, what measures should it adopt to meet the responsibility? The bill does not say what precise measures should be adopted; but it defines a method of procedure for finding out. The method of procedure is defined under the second main heading — The National Production and Employment Budget. The President is required to transmit to

Freedom and Responsibility

Congress at the beginning of each regular session a National Budget, which shall consist of certain statistical information and, if necessary, of certain recommendations. The statistical information shall include: (1) the "estimated size of the labor force, including the self-employed in industry and agriculture"; (2) the "estimated aggregate volume of investment and expenditure by private enterprise, consumers, State and local governments, and the Federal Government" that will be required during the ensuing fiscal year to provide full employment for that labor force; (3) the estimated volume of investment and expenditure by the above-mentioned agencies that will normally be made during the ensuing fiscal year; and (4) the difference between the volume of investment and expenditure that is required and that which will normally be made. So far the Budget is merely a matter of bookkeeping for the ensuing fiscal year. Estimated labor force $=$ X. Estimated investments and expenditures required for employing the labor force $=$ Y. Estimated investments and expenditures by private enterprise, consumers, and governments $=$ Z. If Y and Z are equal, the Budget will balance. If Z is less than Y, the country is headed for depression; if more, it is headed for inflation; and in either case it is the duty of the President to present in the Budget certain "general programs" — programs, as the case may be, for avoiding inflation or for avoiding depression.

If it appears that the country is headed for depression, the President is to present as part of the Budget a general program "designed to stimulate non-Federal investment and expenditure" — a program that "may include, but need not be confined to, current and projected Federal policies and activities with respect to banking and currency, monopoly and competition, wages and working conditions, foreign trade and investments, agriculture, taxation, social security, the development of natural resources, and such

Private Economic Enterprise

other measures as may . . . affect the level of non-Federal investment and expenditure." Should this program be deemed not sufficient, the President shall present another general program "for such Federal investments and expenditures," designed to "contribute to the national wealth and welfare," as will "assure a full employment volume of production." If, on the other hand, it appears that the country is headed for inflation, the President is to present a general program "for preventing inflationary economic dislocations, or diminishing the aggregate volume of investments . . . to the required level, or both." And any program presented shall include such measures as may be necessary to "assure that monopolistic practices with respect to prices, production, or distribution . . . will not interfere with the purposes of this act."

The preparation of the Budget is to be under the general direction and supervision of the President in consultation with the Cabinet and other heads of departments and assisted by such "advisory boards" as he may deem it necessary to create. And, finally, the Budget, having been presented to Congress, is to be turned over to a permanent Joint Committee on the Budget, to be composed of the chairmen and ranking minority members of the Senate committees on Appropriations, Banking and Currency, Education and Labor, and Finance; the chairmen and ranking minority members of the House committees on Appropriations, Banking and Currency, Labor, and Ways and Means; and fourteen additional members of Congress, seven to be appointed by the President of the Senate and seven by the Speaker of the House. The appointments shall be such, however, as "shall reflect the relative membership of the majority and minority parties in the Senate and House of Representatives." The function of the Joint Committee is to examine the Budget and make recommendations for appropriate legislation.

Freedom and Responsibility

Such is the Full Employment Bill. Three points in respect to it are especially worth noting. One is the declaration of national policy. Compared with any declaration of policy that might conceivably have come out of Congress fifteen years ago, that here announced is indeed a radical one. Judged, however, by present-day trends in thought and practice, it is neither radical nor reactionary, but a reasonable compromise between extreme theories of laissez faire and state socialism — reasonable, because it reflects well enough the prevailing opinion in the United States. It places the main emphasis, even with tiresome repetitions, on maintaining and "fostering" private competitive enterprise; and there is no doubt whatever that this is in accord with the opinion of the overwhelming majority of the people of the United States. But it is safe to say that the people, by and large, are coming rapidly and very definitely to feel that prolonged mass unemployment is an intolerable because a preventable situation; that men willing and able to work have a "right to useful, remunerative, regular, and full-time employment"; and that in so far as private enterprise cannot or does not provide such employment "it is the responsibility of the Federal Government" to do whatever is necessary, either by aiding private enterprise or on its own account, to provide it. In this respect the declaration of policy represents very justly what is, or will very shortly be, the prevailing opinion; and since Congress must come to it eventually, it would make for a clarification of the issue if it should now adopt the policy in the explicit and categorical form in which it is expressed in the present bill.

The second point concerns the character and purpose of the National Budget. Such a budget, if taken seriously, could not be prepared by the President and any ordinary corps of assistants working for a couple of months before it had to be presented. It would involve a complete statistical survey of the national economy — a task that would re-

Private Economic Enterprise

quire the services of a large and fully equipped bureau of economic experts permanently employed in gathering and organizing and interpreting the information on which the budget would be based. It would be necessary for the bureau to know month by month and, if called on, to report to the President the fluctuations in employment, in investments and expenditures, the probable coming trend in such matters, and the effectiveness or otherwise of whatever measures may have been taken to maintain a proper level of employment and production. Apart from such constant attention to the national economy as a whole and to the relation of its various parts, it would be impossible to devise and recommend those "general programs" for maintaining "continuing full employment" that the budget calls for. In short, what the National Budget here proposed amounts to is the application of scientific research and the scientific method to legislation. Either it means that or it means nothing of much importance.

The third point concerns the Joint Committee on the National Budget. The committee is required to examine the Budget and report by the first of March. In that time it could not possibly review and check the statistical information on which the conclusions of the Budget are based: it would have to accept the statistical findings or reject them without reason. Almost as little would the committee be able to judge the validity of the programs recommended in the Budget, since these, if they amounted to anything, would be based on the interpretations of the experts whose business it was to understand the intricacies and workings of the national economy: the committee could at best employ other experts to pass upon the conclusions of the first ones. If the Budget were taken as a serious attempt to apply scientific knowledge to legislation, the function of the Joint Committee would be limited to examining the recommended programs, not from the point of view of their inherent merit, but from the point of view of the practical political difficulties of getting particular measures passed through Congress.

The practical political difficulties might indeed be great — so great as to sabotage the experiment and defeat its purposes altogether. But if the experiment were taken seriously and in good faith, the National Budget would of necessity become the central and determining factor in Federal policy and legislation. It would determine in no small measure, or at least be inseparably related to, the policy of the government in respect to banking and currency, foreign trade and investments, taxation, labor conditions and social security, and a great variety of other matters. In that case the Joint Committee would become the central committee of Congress, and it could hardly perform its functions in respect to the Budget without being able to count on the cooperation of the other principal standing committees. A certain integration of such committees with the Joint Committee is achieved by the provisions of the bill that include among the members of the Joint Committee the chairmen and ranking minority members of the leading standing committees of the House and Senate. In so far as the experiment were taken seriously and in so far as it worked, the Joint Committee might then become the starting-point for that "streamlining of Congress," as it is called — that reorganization of the system of Congressional committees and procedures — which is now widely recognized as being highly desirable.

In so far as it worked, the experiment might well have another and very important result. It might very well provide private enterprise with that "confidence" which is now lacking — confidence in the future, reasonable certainty as to what the government might be expected to do, the feeling therefore that it would be good business to take risks, since it could safely count on opportunities — opportuni-

Private Economic Enterprise

ties that would if necessary be underwritten by the government — for business expansion. In so far as such underwriting proved successful in attaining the end desired, the need for it might very well arise less frequently.

In any case, the present bill looks more promising than anything that has yet appeared. It does not provide a specific program, but it seems a sensible way of going about getting one that might work. Its great aim is to maintain "continuing full employment," and it is based on the general assumption that the function of government in achieving that aim is neither to compete with private enterprise nor to place restraints upon it, but merely to provide such assistance as may be necessary to enable it to go ahead and do its proper job.

IN THESE LECTURES, given under a foundation devoted to "American institutions and their preservation," I have discussed the broad fundamental liberties on which American institutions rest, and have suggested from time to time some of the things that are essential to the preservation of those liberties and the institutions created to secure them. Since society is not static, some modification of any set of institutions is always necessary in order to adapt them to the changing conditions in which men live. This is now, as always, necessary; and the more necessary now because of the profound and rapid changes that are occurring. But I hope I have made it clear that something more than the formal modification of our institutions is essential to their preservation. When all is said, what is needed for the solution of the difficult national and international problems that confront us, and therefore for the preservation of our institutions and of the liberties they were created to secure, is more intelligence, more integrity, and a heightened sense of responsibility. We need more intelligence — the knowledge required for understanding the situation and for dealing with it effectively. We need more integrity — less dishonesty and less of the feeling that, in private and in public life, our conscience is clear if we keep, with whatever slick maneuvering, within the letter of the law. But what we need most of all is a heightened sense of individual and collective responsibility — less insistence on negative rights and the unrestrained pursuit of individual self-interest, and a more united and resolute determination to concern ourselves with the public good and to make the sacrifices that are necessary for it.

This is only to say that the preservation of our freedom depends less upon the precise nature of our constitutions and laws than it does upon the character of the people. In the last analysis everything depends upon the possession by the people of that *virtue* (virtue in the ancient Roman sense of the word) which Montesquieu declared to be the fundamental principle, the indispensable guarantee, of the republican form of government.

Index

Abélard, Peter, 29, 59
Abolitionists, 76–7
Alexandria, schools of, 58
American Commonwealth, 20
American Revolution, 11, 68
Aristocracy, decline of, 10–12
Articles of Confederation, 68
Assembly, right of, 79
Associated Press, 79
Athens, 5ff.; schools of, 58

Bagehot, Walter, quoted, 85
Bayle, Pierre, 60
Berkeley, William, 45
Bills of rights, 23, 70, 78ff., 82–3
Bologna, University of, 55
Bradford, William, 7
Bruno, Giordano, 29, 59
Bryce, James, 20f.

Calas, Jean, 29
Charters, colonial, 68
Checks and balances, principle of, 26; in Federal and state constitutions, 73–4
Christian philosophy of history, 58–60
Church, mediaeval, and learning, 58–9
Civil liberties, 78–83; as defined in Constitution of Michigan, 70–2
Collectivism, 96–121
Communism, 96, 100; liberty of teaching concerning, 52–3; in Russia, 102–3; distinguished from Socialism, 103, 106; compared with Fascism, 104–5, 106; with Social Democracy, 106

Communists, and free speech, 35
Compromise of 1850, 77
Connecticut, 8, 68
Connecticut Constitution of 1818, 2, 27, 34
Constitutional government, in U. S., 65–88; virtues of, 83–4; defects of, 84–7
Corn Laws, repeal of, 96
Cotton, John, 8
Crowther, Geoffrey, 113
Curie, Madame, 33
Curie, Pierre, 33

Declaration of Independence, 1, 14, 16, 26, 66, 70
Declaration of the Rights of Man, 3, 14, 26, 90
Decline and Fall of the Roman Empire, 17
Democracy, 32, 35; obstacles to, 38–41; and freedom of learning and teaching, 45, 62–4
Democracy, Western and Southern, triumph of, 11–12
Dennis, Lawrence, trial of, 80
Depression, great, 21
Dictatorships, 63; downfall of, 64

Economic theory, and vested interests, 61–2
Einstein, Albert, 49
Emporia Gazette, 41
England, freedom of mind in, 29
Equality, 9ff., 17
Erasmus, Desiderius, 60
Ex parte Mitsuye Endo, 80

i

Index

"Factory acts," English, 96–7
Fascism, 1, 96, 100, 103–5; compared with Communism, 104–5, 106; with Social Democracy and Socialism, 106; dangerous character of, 109; possible American brand of, 109–10
Fascists, and free speech, 35
Federal Constitution, 2, 16, 68; tenth amendment to, 23; as model of state constitutions, 69; dispersion of political power by, 73–4; changes in, 74; need for revision of, 87; see also Bills of rights
Free enterprise, 77, 92–3, 108
Free lands, 9ff.
Freedom of learning and teaching, 43, 44–64, 105; philosophical justification of, 46–50; practical justification of, 56–62
Freedom of religion, 9, 30, 105; in England, 29; as defined in Constitution of Michigan, 70–1
Freedom of speech, 2, 4, 27–43, 105; in practice, 34, 40–1, 79; and social evils, 36; abuses of, 36–8; as defined in Constitution of Michigan, 70
Freedom of Speech and of the press, 33
Freedom of the mind, 27–64
Freedom of the press, 2, 3–4, 27–43, 105; in practice, 34, 40–1, 79
Freedom, political, meaning of, 65–6
French Revolution, 90
Frontier, and freedom, 8–9, 12
Full Employment bill, 114–21

Galilei, Galileo, 29, 60
German language, teaching of, forbidden, 53
Germany, 63, 103ff.
Gibbon, Edward, 17, 60
Goethe, Johann Wolfgang von, 6

Governmental regulation of business, 96–100
Greeks, ancient, 49

Hellenic age, 58
Hitler, Adolf, 6, 104
Hobbes, Thomas, 64
Homestead Act, 98
Hooker, Thomas, 8
Hutchinson, Anne, 8

Immigration, reasons for, 6–7
Indiana Constitution of 1816, 45, 51
Industrial revolution, 93–4
Italy, 63, 103f.

Jackson, Andrew, election of, 11
Japanese-American citizens, trial of, 80
Jefferson, Thomas, 14–15, 16, 18, 27, 30, 32, 41, 46, 66, 70, 94; on tyranny of majority, 25–6
Justification by faith, doctrine of, 13

Kepler, Johann, 60

Laissez faire, see Private economic enterprise
Liberal-democratic revolution, 60–1
Liberty: defined, 3, 37; in Germany, 4; in Russia, 4–5
Lyttleton, Oliver, 113

Majority: will of, 23–5, 66–7, 70; tyranny of, 25–6
Managed economy, 96
Marx, Karl, 52–3, 100, 102
Marxian philosophy, 100–2, 103
Massachusetts Bay, 8
Middle West, 9; as political force, 11–12
Mill, James, 31–2
Mill, John Stuart, 31–2
Minority, 24f.; rights of, 67
Montesquieu, de, Charles de Secondat, 122

Index

Morrison, Herbert, 113
Murray-Kilgore bill, 114–21
Mussolini, Benito, 27, 104

Natural law, 61; in eighteenth century, 30–1; today, 41–2
Natural rights, 13–17, 26, 28; in Declaration of Independence, 14, 16; in America and Europe, compared, 16–17
Negroes, 18
New Deal, 99
New Freedom, 99
New Learning, 60
Newspaper press, 40–1
Newton, Isaac, 29
Newtown, 8
New York, western, 9

Paine, Thomas, 5
Paris, University of, 55
Pennsylvania, 9
People: will of, 23–4; sovereignty of, 65–6, 69–70; *see also* Majority, will of
Plato, 49, 105
Political liberties, 105–6
Political parties, 84
Poore, B. P., 69
Private economic enterprise, 89–121; right of, 89–91, 106; and laissez faire, 91–5; regulation of, 96–100, 111
Private property, *see* Private economic enterprise
Prohibition, 87
Propaganda, instruments of, 41

Radio, 40, 79
Reason, 31–2, 42
Reformation, Protestant, 13
Regulation of business, governmental, 96–100
Revival of learning, 58
Rhode Island, 8, 68
Rome, ancient, learning in, 58

Roosevelt, Theodore, 99
Rousseau, Jean Jacques, 24
Russia, 63
Russian Revolution of October 1917, 102f.

Saturday Review of Literature, 79
Schools, freedom of teaching in, 51–5
Science and theology, conflict between, 60f.
Self-government, *see* Democracy
Separation of powers, principle of, 73, 87
Slavery controversy, 76–7
Smith, Adam, 90
Social compact, 24
Social Democracy, 96–100, 103; compared with Socialism, Communism, and Fascism, 106; how to achieve, 110–21
Social legislation, in England, 97; in U. S., 97–8
Socialism, 96, 100, 102; distinguished from Communism, 103, 106; compared with Social Democracy and Fascism, 106
Socrates: as teacher, 55–6; trial of, 57f.
Sovereignty of people, *see* People
Spain, 103
State constitutions, 16, 68f.
Strange Fruit, 79
Sumerians, 49

Taine, H. A., 69
Technological revolution, 93–4
Texas Constitution of 1845, quoted, 66
Trial by jury, right of: as defined in Constitution of Michigan, 70; in practice, 81–2
Trial, fair and speedy, right to: as defined in Constitution of Michigan, 70; in practice, 80
Tübingen, University of, 60

Index

Universities: origin of, 55–6; functions of, 56; and political community, 57–8; in mediaeval period, 58–9; in early modern period, 59–60; since eighteenth century, 60–2

Veblen, Thorstein, 61–2
Virginia, 9
Volney, C. F., 30–1
Voltaire, F. M. A. de, 33; and freedom of mind, 28–30

"Wave of the future," 63f.
Wealth of Nations, 90
White, William Allen, 41
William of Occam, 59
Williams, Roger, 8
Wilson, Woodrow, 99; on inflexibility of American system of government, quoted, 85
Winthrop, John, 7
World revolution, 77

Date Due

ENNIS AND NANCY HAM LIBRARY
ROCHESTER COLLEGE
800 WEST AVON ROAD
ROCHESTER HILLS, MI 48307